"MALE AND FEMALE HE CREATED THEM"

JORGE CARDINAL MEDINA ESTÉVEZ

"Male and Female He Created Them"

On Marriage and the Family

Translated by
Eladia Gomez-Posthill
and
Michael J. Miller

IGNATIUS PRESS   SAN FRANCISCO

Original Spanish edition:
"Y los creo varon y mujer":
Escritos sobre el matrimonio y la familia
©1997 Ediciones Universidad Católica de Chile
Santiago, Chile

Unless otherwise noted, all Scripture quotations (except those included within the patristic texts themselves) have been taken from the Revised Standard Version of the Holy Bible, the Old Testament © 1952, the Apocrypha © 1957, the New Testament © 1946, by the Division of Christian Education of the National Council of the Churches of Christ in the United States of America; New Catholic Edition, Revised Standard Version, 2003.

Excerpts from the English translation of the *Catechism of the Catholic Church* for use in the United States of America copyright © 1994, United States Catholic Conference, Inc.—Libreria Editrice Vaticana. English translation of the *Catechism of the Catholic Church: Modifications from the Editio Typica* copyright © 1997, United States Catholic Conference, Inc.—Libreria Editrice Vaticana.

Cover art: *Creation of Adam and Eve* (detail)
Lorenzo Ghiberti
Panel from *The Gates of Paradise*, 1425–1452
Museo dell'Opera del Duomo, Florence, Italy
Copyright Alinari/Art Resource, New York

Cover design by Roxanne Mei Lum

© 2003 Ignatius Press, San Francisco
All rights reserved
ISBN 0–89870–943–1
Library of Congress Control Number 2002112868
Printed in the United States of America ∞

Contents

Abbreviations

CCC   *Catechism of the Catholic Church*

CIC   *Codex Iuris Canonici*, 1983

DS   Denzinger-Schonmetzer, *Enchiridion Symbolorum,*
        definitionum et declarationum de rebus fidei et morum

GS   Vatican II. *Gaudium et spes.* December 7, 1965.

FC   Pope John Paul II. *Familiaris consortio.* November 2, 1981.

LG   Vatican II. *Lumen gentium.* November 21, 1964.

PART ONE

"MALE AND FEMALE HE CREATED THEM"

(Genesis 1:27)

A FEW WORDS...

Various pastoral needs that I have encountered in different areas of priestly ministry have convinced me that it would be useful to write a short work on the sacrament of matrimony. Marriage is, after all, a subject that is always of current interest, something that touches the very heart of the Church's life.

My purpose in writing the following pages was the same one that guided me in other short works that I have published: to set forth Catholic doctrine with fidelity and precision, leaving aside opinions and matters about which Catholics are free to disagree.

May God bless the young, and the not-so-young, who kindly devote part of their time to reading these pages, which were affectionately written for them with deep pastoral concern and the awareness that what is said here could be said much better. I have in mind a great many persons, to whom these pages are dedicated.

My wish is that this little work, the fruit of some leisure time during a vacation, might be a homage to the fiftieth anniversary of the publication of the Encyclical *Casti Connubii* of Pope Pius XI, dated December 31, 1930, on Christian marriage, and also to the Synod of Bishops on this topic which was held last year with the Holy Father presiding— Pope John Paul II, who governs the Church surrounded by the love and fidelity of his children.

FEBRUARY 1981

This prologue is a preface to this first text, which is the most extensive work included in this anthology. Although many of the themes that it takes up are treated in greater detail in other documents, we have preferred to reprint it in its entirety, so that it would not lose its character of a connected discourse addressed especially to those who are about to be married— Joaquín García-Huidobro, ED.

CHAPTER ONE

This Is a Great Mystery, in Christ and in the Church

[Ephesians 5:32]

Christian Marriage

I. Introduction

No human institution is so deeply rooted in nature and in the heart of man and of woman as marriage and the family. Prior to any philosophical reasoning, men and women know that they are made for each other, that they need each other, and that there exists between them a sort a relationship that is different from all the other relationships found in human society.

The name given to this relationship is *love*, and to it artists throughout the ages have devoted works of great beauty, seeking in it their inspiration for music, dance, poetry, literature, painting, and sculpture. This is an unequivocal sign that love is a dimension of human existence that flows from a most noble wellspring, capable of giving rise to profound joys, sustaining great efforts, and enduring difficult sacrifices.

The history of the most ancient civilizations always provides data about the institution of marriage, through which we can detect, albeit with many imperfections, a nostalgic yearning for an ideal of love that is fully considerate, faithful, and tender. More than a few studies of peoples that to this day have preserved certain aboriginal characteristics confirm they have an exalted concept of marriage and family, a concept expressed in customs of greater integrity than those that exist, or are accepted, among nations that call themselves "civilized".

This most noble institution, however, like all the rest of human existence, bears the disruptive and debasing marks of sin. The disordered sexual appetite has distorted the relationship of love between man and woman, to the point where the word "love" is used nowadays to describe situations that have little or nothing to do with the profound experience that the term implies. The word "love" is sometimes used in ways that are truly a sacrilege or at least a *deformed and grotesque caricature*.

These customs and attitudes all have something in common: the dignity of the person is reduced to the level of a thing or object; the man and the woman "use" or "exploit" each other, they make themselves objects of commerce in various ways—in short, they debase themselves. A "price" is set on something that is priceless; "profits" are gained from what is, by its very nature, free and gratuitous, and people fall into the error of believing that a passing emotion, or lewd sensuality, or a relationship of pleasure completely devoid of sacrifice, deserves the name of love.

In general, although not exclusively, it is the woman who ends up being wounded more visibly, even if the man who hurts her is also deeply wounded by making himself incapable of showing respect, the only attitude that corresponds to his dignity.

It would be very time-consuming to take an inventory of the degradation of love, but it is not irrelevant to recall some of its manifestations. Not all of them display the same characteristics, but all are, in one form or another, deviations from true love. Some of them provoke universal condemnation; it is disgraceful that others are accepted as something normal or at least as a lesser evil.

Antiquity saw the existence of *polygamy* on a vast scale: a man could have several women. Whether this occurred as an expression of prestige and power, or as a means of multiplying family alliances, or from a desire for numerous offspring, or simply out of concupiscence, there is no doubt that polygamy dealt a serious blow to love and to the equality between man and woman. Though more rare, the phenomenon of *polyandry*, in which several men possess one and the same woman, was also known.

Repudiation, or *divorce*, is also known from ancient times. Whether it was because one of the spouses, usually the woman, had committed a transgression, or because she was thought to be infertile, or due to discord and disagreements, or simply because he desired a younger or more beautiful woman, the husband would abandon his first wife in order to take another. Sometimes divorce was considered a "merciful" solution, since otherwise some men might have opted to take the life of the spouse who was bothersome or displeasing.

Adultery has a long history. On an occasional or ongoing basis, a married person has illicit relations with someone other than his or her spouse, usually while keeping the arrangement secret, although at times this is made blatantly and shamelessly public and may even be tolerated or accepted by the faithful spouse. An innocuous expression has been coined to describe the adulterer who is involved in ongoing adultery: he or she is called a "lover", as if adultery could ever be decked out in the apparel of true love.

Prostitution is an old form of this degradation of love. The poor girl who, usually because of poverty, offers her body as a commodity with which to "make love" (what a monstrous misuse of the word!) is prey to whoever can "pay" for her services, to a man who does not love her and will never love her—who, in fact, scorns her and sees nothing in her but flesh. When there is a shortage in this human traffic, which is not that different from the slavery of antiquity, the suppliers will resort to all kinds of contrivances, and a whole system of "export" and "import" will be put into play to satisfy a market that is always willing to pay handsomely for its human merchandise. The "white slave trade" is not, unfortunately, a tale from the past.

Some will speak of, and engage in, so-called *"free love"*. This means sharing a body as one shares a meal, or friendship, or any other thing. It is as if the relationship between the man and the woman were, with a greater or lesser tinge of affection or permanence, nothing more than the satisfaction of a need to which both parties lend themselves "obligingly", without any commitment or responsibility. It lasts for as long as it lasts. It is based on a twofold error, since it acknowledges neither what love is nor what freedom is.

Others engage in *"premarital relations"*. Whether because it is not possible to get married right away, or because the excuse is made that "we're in love", or else because "proofs of love" are demanded and given, or because the couple want to be sure about their sexual compatibility before getting married, or because such activity is considered less vicious than, say, masturbation or resorting to prostitution—what is certain is that this form of conduct is spreading at an alarming rate. Worse yet, it is excused and defended to the point of being considered normal and morally irreproachable.

Aside from polygamy and divorce, all the other deviations have something in common: the fear that a new life may arise from the relationship. Neither the adulterer nor the lover, the prostitute nor the engaged couples who are having sexual relations want a child; they are afraid of him, they avoid him, they kill him before he is born, or, in a cowardly way, they ignore him afterward or deny responsibility. One must admit that in these attitudes they demonstrate neither responsibility nor courage. If the woman defends the baby in her womb and brings him into the world, in certain circles people will point at her or persuade her to get rid of him privately, because she has "lost her reputation"—as though making paternity less evident made the father more honorable! If there were less hypocrisy, we would extend a helping hand to the woman who, due to error, ignorance, or weakness, conceived a child and had the courage to welcome him and give him a mother's love, even when the father—a man, but no gentleman—slips away into the shadows of irresponsibility disguised with "respectability".

We could list still other degradations of love, or rather debaucheries of the sexual appetite. Sometimes *incest* occurs, between persons who are closely related or occasionally, sad to say, between members of the same family. Then there is *sexual abuse of minors*, innocent victims of abnormal concupiscence. Some engage in *erotic foreplay*, the dangerous antechambers to more serious acts. There are forms of *homosexual activity*, often bordering on psychological abnormality.

The reader may have found that the preceding paragraphs make disagreeable reading. What sense is there in starting a study on marriage with a catalogue of the miseries that disfigure and degrade it or which are more or less crude counterfeits of love? Would it not be better to begin by showing the positive side and to disregard in print what everybody knows in fact?

We have started with this unpleasant inventory because we believe that it is beneficial to recall that the eminent dignity of love and marriage is as beautiful as it is fragile, and that the human heart, in this field as in so many others, experiences the terrible sting of sin. It would be unrealistic to paint an idyllic or romantic picture of love, when experience shows us that the facts deviate so lamentably from the human and Christian ideal. So please excuse us for having caused such a shock! The shadows serve only to emphasize more clearly the radiance and beauty of the Christian and Catholic message concerning love, marriage, and the family.

The pages that follow are meant to be a service offered in the first place to those who hold the Catholic faith, to help them to remember the doctrine of the Church on love, marriage, and the family. I have in mind so many young people who are planning to start a family and who need clarity so as not to give in to confusion and error. I am thinking also of my brothers and sisters in the faith who have already contracted marriage but need to deepen their understanding of it and need to guide their children. Perhaps these words could help some catechist or other brothers in the ministry, for instance, deacons or priests.

Of course, I am grateful to so many married friends of mine who have helped me by their example, have encouraged me to put these reflections into writing, have told me about their experiences of Christian conjugal life and, by their lives, confirm the conviction that marriage is a source of genuine happiness and a path to holiness, when it is lived in faith, in love, and in sacrifice.

II. Marriage in the Old Testament

Origins

The first book of the Bible, Genesis, contains the fundamental teaching on marriage. Let us read some passages:

So God created man in his own image, in the image of God he created him; male and female he created them. And God blessed them, and God said to them, "Be fruitful and multiply, and fill the earth and subdue it; and have dominion over the fish of the sea and over the birds of the air and over every living thing that moves upon the earth" (Gen 1:27–28).

There is another, more extensive passage, that says:

The man gave names to all cattle, and to the birds of the air, and to every beast of the field; but for the man there was not found a helper fit for him. So the LORD God caused a deep sleep to fall upon the man, and while he slept took one of his ribs and closed up its place with flesh; and the rib which the LORD God had taken from the man he made into a woman and brought her to the man. Then the man said,

> "This at last is bone of my bones
>   and flesh of my flesh;
> she shall be called Woman,
>   because she was taken out of Man."

Therefore a man leaves his father and his mother and cleaves to his wife, and they become one flesh. And the man and his wife were both naked, and were not ashamed (Gen 2:20–24).

These two passages, which refer to man's situation before his sin, teach us a number of things:
— that man is an image of God and one of his works;
— that the difference between the sexes is God's work;
— that the reason for this difference is the propagation of the human race and mutual assistance;
— that woman has the same dignity as man;
— that the union between man and woman is so deep that it surpasses even that which exists between parents and children; and finally,

— that before sin there was no sexual disorder, which is expressed in shame at one's nakedness.

We can imagine that the man was enthusiastic and happy to find his companion in life; he understood that his union with her was not something transitory and fleeting, and that she, silently, welcomed the first manifestations of his tenderness and responded to them. Great artists such as Albrecht Dürer and Michelangelo have expressed the harmony of the original state of the man and the woman. In the parish church of Malmö, in Sweden, there is a beautiful medieval tableau depicting Adam and Eve naked in paradise.

We will not dwell on the biblical account of original sin (this can be found in Gen 3:1ff.), but rather on the consequences that it had for the human couple.

The Bible tells us that "the eyes of both were opened, and they knew that they were naked; and they sewed fig leaves together and made themselves aprons" (Gen 3:7), and that when they heard God looking for them, they hid from him (verse 8). When God called to the man and asked him where he was, the man replied, "I heard the sound of you in the garden, and I was afraid, because I was naked" (Gen 3:10).

Original innocence was gone, and man and woman began to experience a disruption of the sexual order, expressed in shame. This sense of shame would be from then on a curb on the sexual appetite, and it is the foundation of the *Christian virtue of modesty*, which seeks to avoid that which in one sex is an incentive to disorder for the other. We cannot forget that in our present condition, after original sin and burdened with its consequences, the natural harmony that existed between the sexes before original sin is no longer possible.

Hence it is an illusion to believe that there can be between men and women, after original sin, such a healthy relationship as to be carefree, as if concupiscence did not exist, or as if there were human beings so "angelic" that they did not experience sexual passion. The natural thing for us today is to *guard against and master* the impulses of our fallen nature. The forms of modesty can change, but there must always be some: clothes, distances, attitudes, and reserve, which are expressions of interior purity and of the charitable intention to avoid provocation.

But sin had other consequences for family life, too. When the man was asked by God why he had disobeyed, he found no better excuse than to blame "the woman whom you gave to be with me" (Gen 3:12). She, who had been created to be his helpmate, for his happiness and well-being, is now accused of being the cause of his ruin. Misunderstanding, mistrust, and deception are born. And chastisement came from God, who said to the woman,

> "I will greatly multiply your pain in childbearing;
>   in pain you shall bring forth children,
> yet your desire shall be for your husband,
>   and he shall rule over you" (Gen 3:16).

Motherhood became painful, and the woman discovered that she was capable of seeking man in a disordered way, falling into the snare of *his* power, whereas he was capable of relegating her to the margin of love. The original human community was wounded, and from then on harmony and mutual respect would no longer be a spontaneous fruit of the natural state blessed by God, but rather the painstaking and arduous result of the self-control that each one would exercise over his impulses.

Sacred Scripture adds, after this sad episode, "And the LORD God made for Adam and for his wife garments of skins, and clothed them" (Gen 3:21), as if he wanted to underscore the insufficiency of their first garment of leaves and the need to cultivate modesty.

Humanly speaking, what happened was a "disaster" for God and the downfall of man. It was enough to make a person lose heart. However, God has a big heart, and he was not resigned to seeing his work spoiled definitively. It would be a long road ahead, but he was going to restore the human couple to their dignity, and to this task he devoted so many words, so much patience, and so much love.

Lights and Shadows

Through the centuries, and as a consequence of sin, the original purity and harmony of marriage suffered grievous harm but were not entirely obscured.

Polygamy appeared, and it was practiced among the people of Israel without anyone considering it morally objectionable. The Bible mentions Lamech, a descendent of Cain, as the first man who took two wives (Gen 4:19). The patriarch Jacob had four wives (Gen 35:23–25).

It was in Jacob's family that the first case of *incest* occurred (Gen 35:22), a situation that was to be repeated between a son of Jacob, Judah, and his daughter-in-law, Tamar (Gen 38:15–26). A son of Judah was the first to *avoid having children* by interrupting the sexual act (Gen 38:9). King David was polygamous, and yet he stained himself with the crime of *adultery*, taking the wife of a neighbor of his, whose death he arranged (2 Sam 11), for which the prophet Nathan rebuked him severely in the name of God (2 Sam 12), who punished him with the death of the son conceived in adultery.

The Bible mentions the existence of *prostitution* (Gen 38:15; Josh 2:1). David's son, King Solomon, also was polygamous and took many foreign wives, contrary to the precepts of

God. These women dragged him down into idolatry, and then, for love of them, he consented to have places of worship established for the false gods that they adored (1 Kings 11:1–13). Because of the hardness of man's heart, Moses permitted *divorce* among the people of Israel (Deut 24:1–4) but, at the same time, denounced and severely forbade many sexual abuses that existed and were being practiced among the neighboring peoples: *incest, adultery, homosexuality,* and *performing the sexual act with animals* (Lev 18:6–30).

Those peoples developed a custom of "sacred prostitution", in which prostitutes carried on their activity as part of the worship of false gods. One can scarcely imagine such an aberration. Homosexuality enjoyed enormous popularity in Sodom (from which homosexuality acquired the name of "sodomy"), and for that reason God destroyed the city by making fire from heaven rain down upon it (Gen 19:1–29).

It was not all darkness and abuses, however. The Bible describes the *purity of Joseph*, son of Jacob, who categorically rejected the propositions of the married Egyptian woman who had bought him as a slave. That rejection earned him the calumny of the scorned woman, who had him incarcerated (Gen 39:7–20). The Book of Ruth tells of a most beautiful and *delicate love* between her and Boaz, who were ancestors of Jesus Christ (Ruth 3 and 4).

The Song of Solomon [Canticle of Canticles], the summit of the Bible's lyrical poetry, has as its theme a delicate and refined love that is intertwined with beautiful sentiments. Psalm 45 (numbered 44 in the Vulgate Bible) is a nuptial song that exalts love and fertility. These texts indicate that, despite so many deviations, *the ideal of love* was still very much alive.

The "sapiential" books of the Bible, so called because they contain reflections upon the wisdom of the Hebrew people, refer quite frequently to *woman, marriage, purity, fidelity,* and *the education of children* (see, for example, Prov 5:1–19; 6:20–34; 7:7–25; 28:15–17; Eccles 3:1–18; 7:25–30; 9:1–13; 22:3–6; 23:21–37; 25:24–35; 26:1–34; 30:1–13; 36:23–28; 42:9–11). The happiness of a home with a diligent woman at the heart of it is described in the Book of Proverbs, chapter 31, verses 10 to 31. Naturally, some of these passages reflect a situation that was still very distant from the fullness of the gospel, but on the whole they testify to sound and lofty ideals. A Christian can benefit from reading them and meditating on them.

One of the most beautiful pages on marriage in the Old Testament is the short Book of Tobit. It is the story of a God-fearing household, noted for its works of charity but also tested by tribulation, whose son contracts marriage with a girl who is related to him, whom he meets along the mysterious paths of God's Providence. I highly recommend reading it in its entirety, especially for those who are engaged. Let us read now a passage from this book, in which are manifested the profound religious sentiments with which the young man enters into marriage:

> When the door was shut and the two were alone, Tobias got up from the bed and said, "Sister, get up, and let us pray and implore our Lord that he grant us mercy and safety." And Tobias began to pray,
>
> > "Blessed are you, O God of our fathers,
> > and blessed be your holy and glorious name for ever.
> > Let the heavens and all your creatures bless you.
> > You made Adam and gave him Eve his wife
> > as a helper and support.
> > From them the race of mankind has sprung.
> > You said, 'It is not good that the man should be alone;
> > let us make a helper for him like himself.'
>
> And now, O Lord, I am not taking this sister of mine because of lust, but with sincerity. Grant that I may find mercy and

may grow old together with her." And they both said, "Amen, amen." Then they both went to sleep for the night (Tob 8:4–9).

The sentiments of Sarah's parents, Tobias' father- and mother-in-law, are expressed with a moving simplicity and wisdom:

> He said also to his daughter, "Honor your father-in-law and your mother-in-law; they are now your parents. Let me hear a good report of you." And he kissed her. And Edna said to Tobias, "The Lord of heaven bring you back safely, dear brother, and grant me to see your children by my daughter Sarah, that I may rejoice before the Lord. See, I am entrusting my daughter to you; do nothing to grieve her" (Tob 10:12 RSV).

This beautiful book from the Bible is very important because it emphasizes the *spiritual significance* of marriage. It shows a marriage realized in the presence of God, a marriage impregnated with a religious sense, which begins with prayer and includes an apostolic dimension (see Tob 13:1–18). This explains the advice of Tobias' father to his son: "Beware, my son, of all immorality" (Tob 4:12), since impurity has nothing to do with true love. It was God who arranged for Tobias and Sarah to meet, and in him and for him they loved one another and had children. Each one was for the other, in love and fidelity.

A Still Brighter Light

In two books of the Old Testament—Hosea and Ezekiel—the theme of marriage serves to describe the covenant of love between God and his people Israel: God presents himself as the spouse of his people, inasmuch as this people is described as an unfaithful spouse. Israel's infidelity, its "adultery" and "fornication" as the Bible calls it, consists in abandoning the true God and worshipping false gods. God punishes his unfaithful people but does not abandon them forever: his love, though insulted and mocked, continues to be faithful.

Here is the passage—of great literary beauty and full of lessons—from the Book of Ezekiel:

"And as for your birth, on the day you were born [God says to Israel] your navel string was not cut, nor were you washed with water to cleanse you, nor rubbed with salt, nor swathed with bands. No eye pitied you, to do any of these things to you out of compassion for you; but you were cast out on the open field, for you were abhorred, on the day that you were born.

"And when I passed by you, and saw you weltering in your blood, I said to you in your blood, 'Live, and grow up like a plant of the field.' And you grew up and became tall and arrived at full maidenhood . . . yet you were naked and bare.

"When I passed by you again and looked upon you, behold, you were at the age for love; and I spread my skirt over you, and covered your nakedness: yes, I pledged myself to you and entered into a covenant with you, says the Lord GOD, and you became mine. Then I bathed you with water and washed off your blood from you, and anointed you with oil. I clothed you also with embroidered cloth and shod you with leather, I wrapped you in fine linen and covered you with silk. And I decked you with ornaments, and put bracelets on your arms, and a chain on your neck. And I put a ring on your nose, and earrings in your ears, and a beautiful crown upon your head. Thus you were decked with gold and silver; and your clothing was of fine linen, and silk, and embroidered cloth; you ate fine flour and honey and oil. You grew exceedingly beautiful, and came to regal estate. And your renown went forth among the nations because of your beauty, for it was perfect through the splendor which I had bestowed upon you, says the Lord GOD.

"But you trusted in your beauty, and played the harlot because of your renown, and lavished your harlotries on any passer-by. You took . . . your fair jewels of my gold and of my silver, which I had given you, and made for yourself images of men, and with them played the harlot . . . And you took your sons and your daughters, whom you had borne to me, and these you sacrificed to them [to the idols] to be devoured. . . . And in all your abominations and your harlotries you did not remember the days of your youth. . . .

"How lovesick is your heart, says the Lord GOD, seeing you did all these things, the deeds of a brazen harlot . . . And I will judge you as women who break wedlock and shed blood are judged, and bring upon you the blood of wrath and jealousy. . . . Yes, thus says the Lord GOD . . . yet I will remember my covenant with you in the days of your youth, and I will establish with you an everlasting covenant. . . . I will establish my covenant with you, and you shall know that I am the LORD" (Ezek 16:4–63, excerpts; see also Hos 2:4–25).

This scriptural passage aims to show the gravity of Israel's religious unfaithfulness. Of interest here, however, is the fact that, in order to make even clearer the seriousness of that sin, the passage presents it under the form of marital infidelity. It presupposes a *teaching about marriage*, in that it stresses the immense importance of mutual fidelity between spouses. There are also other elements which are noted in passing, for example, fertility and the consecration of one's children to God, since they are engendered for him. God does not resort to divorcing his people, contrary to what Moses had allowed spouses to do. He adheres instead to an absolute fidelity, because he does not repent of his love.

Thus we find a twofold comparison: first, the love of God for Israel is likened to conjugal love and, vice versa, conjugal love is compared to the steadfast love of God for his people. No doubt, in this passage there are various elements that reflect the customs in antiquity and the love of a prince for a poor girl. But aside from these elements, which are part of the pageantry of literature, there is a profound religious message that was valid then and always will be.

This passage from Ezekiel heralds almost to the letter the perspective which the Apostle Paul will set forth in the New Testament, as we shall see further on.

III. Marriage in the New Testament

The Teaching of Jesus

In Jesus' time, the great majority of the Jews lived in monogamous marriages, that is to say, one man with one woman. There had been a notorious case of adultery, however, that of the petty king Herod, who had taken his brother's wife. John the Baptist, that austere and courageous prophet, made it known to Herod in no uncertain terms that this was unacceptable. His holy intransigence cost him dearly; the king, giving in to passion, silenced John forever. He ordered his execution and had his head delivered as a trophy to the provocative girl who asked for it at the instigation of the adulteress (Mt 14:3–12; Mk 6:17–29). It is interesting to note that John the Baptist died *a martyr for defending the indissolubility of marriage.*

It was precisely the issue of the indissolubility of marriage that some of the Jews put to Jesus:

> And Pharisees came up and in order to test him [Jesus] asked, "Is it lawful for a man to divorce his wife?" He answered them, "What did Moses command you?" They said, "Moses

allowed a man to write a certificate of divorce, and to put her away." But Jesus said to them, "For your hardness of heart he wrote you this commandment. But from the beginning of creation, 'God made them male and female.' 'For this reason a man shall leave his father and mother and be joined to his wife, and the two shall become one.' So they are no longer two but one flesh. What therefore God has joined together, let not man put asunder."

And in the house the disciples asked him again about this matter. And he said to them, "Whoever divorces his wife and marries another, commits adultery against her; and if she divorces her husband and marries another, she commits adultery" (Mk 10:2–12; see also Mt 19:3–9).

"Every one who divorces his wife and marries another commits adultery, and he who marries a woman divorced from her husband commits adultery" (Lk 16:18).

"It was also said, 'Whoever divorces his wife, let him give her a certificate of divorce.' But I say to you that every one who divorces his wife, except on the ground of unchastity, makes her an adulteress; and whoever marries a divorced woman commits adultery" (Mt 5:31–32).

Jesus' words are clear and unequivocal. But he was even more exacting: "You have heard that it was said [in the Ten Commandments], 'You shall not commit adultery.' But I say to you that every one who looks at a woman lustfully has already committed adultery with her in his heart" (Mt 5:27–28).

There can be no doubt that Jesus has a lofty concept of marriage. His teaching is rooted in that of the Old Testament but rejects the leniency introduced by Moses, and demands that marriage conform to the original law that God devised for it when he created man and woman. That is why he quotes Genesis 2:24, just as, centuries before, the Book of Tobit had done. He not only rejects the act of adultery, but also demands of his disciples purity of intention and chastity of heart. Without these, mere external "correctness" would be insufficient in God's eyes.

Yet Jesus also underscores the transitory character of marriage: conjugal relations, though lawful and sacred within marriage, belong only to our pilgrimage here on earth: "The sons of this age marry and are given in marriage; but those who are accounted worthy to attain to that age [to eternal life] and to the resurrection from the dead neither marry nor are given in marriage, for they cannot die any more, because they are equal to angels and are sons of God, being sons of the resurrection" (Lk 20:34–36; see also Mt 22:29–30; Mk 12:25).

The theme of God as the Spouse of his people, initiated by the prophets Hosea and Ezekiel, is applied to Jesus by John the Baptist: "I am not the Christ, but I have been sent before him. He who has the bride is the bridegroom; the friend of the bridegroom, who stands and hears him, rejoices greatly at the bridegroom's voice; therefore this joy of mine is now full. He [Jesus] must increase, but I must decrease" (Jn 3:28–30). Jesus himself claimed the title of spouse in an explicit way (Mt 9:15) and suggested it in several parables (Mt 22:1–13; 25:1–13).

Although it is certain that Jesus showed mercy to the Samaritan woman who had had five husbands and was living with a sixth man who was not her husband (Jn 4:4–19) and to the adulterous woman (Jn 8:1–11), that mercy *in no way implies a compromise with impurity*. His final words to the poor adulteress prove it: "Go, and do not sin again" (Jn 8:11).

The Teaching of Saint Paul

The Letter of Saint Paul to the Ephesians contains a passage that has become a classic as an epitome of Christian doctrine on marriage:

Wives, be subject to your husbands, as to the Lord. For the husband is the head of the wife as Christ is the head of the Church, his body, and is himself its Savior. As the Church is subject to Christ, so let wives also be subject in everything to their husbands. Husbands, love your wives, as Christ loved the Church and gave himself up for her, that he might sanctify her, having cleansed her by the washing of water [baptism] with the word [of the Gospel], that he might present the Church to himself in splendor, without spot or wrinkle or any such thing, that she might be holy and without blemish. Even so husbands should love their wives as their own bodies. He who loves his wife loves himself. For no man ever hates his own flesh, but nourishes and cherishes it, as Christ does the Church, because we are members of his body. "For this reason a man shall leave his father and mother and be joined to his wife, and the two shall become one flesh." This is a great mystery, and I mean in reference to Christ and the Church; however, let each one of you love his wife as himself, and let the wife see that she respects her husband (Eph 5:22–33).

In this rich, sublime passage several teachings about Christian marriage can be inferred:

— The Christian union between husband and wife *represents the covenant of love that exists between Christ and the Church.*
— This union extends *beyond the natural plane*, since it is a mystery of sanctification, as is the union of Christ with the Church.
— The husband's *authority* as head of the household must be *modeled on that of Christ*: a loving, tender, delicate authority.
— The wife's *respect* for her husband must also be modeled on the Church's devotion to Christ: *the fruit of love* and not of fear.

Yet the element that truly stands out in this beautiful passage by Saint Paul is the concept of marriage as a *spiritual and supernatural reality*, a means of sanctification that strengthens the union of each of the spouses with Christ. Thus marriage appears, for the first time, as an explicit *path to sanctity*, further developing the vision already suggested by the Book of Tobit.

This understanding explains why Saint Paul ascribed such *great honor to a first and only marriage* (1 Tim 3:2, 12; 5:9; see Tit 1:6), because in it the undivided love of Christ for his Church shines with a special radiance. The Apostle, however, *did not prohibit or belittle remarriage after widowhood* (1 Tim 5:14)—"A wife is bound to her husband as long as he lives. If the husband dies, she is free to be married to whom she wishes, only in the Lord. But in my judgment she is happier if she remains as she is. And I think that I have the Spirit of God" (1 Cor 7:39–40).

On a more practical level, and because of the strength of the sexual urge, the Apostle says:

> It is well for a man not to touch a woman. But because of the temptation to immorality, each man should have his own wife and each woman her own husband. The husband should give to his wife her conjugal rights, and likewise the wife to her husband. For the wife does not rule over her own body, but the husband does; likewise the husband does not rule over his own body, but the wife does. Do not refuse one another except perhaps by agreement for a season, that you may devote yourselves to prayer; but then come together again, lest Satan tempt you through lack of self-control (1 Cor 7:1–5).

As for the indissolubility of marriage, Saint Paul's teaching could not be any clearer: "To the married I give charge, not I but the Lord, that the wife should not separate from her husband (but if she does, let her remain single or else be reconciled to her husband)—and that the husband should not divorce his wife" (1 Cor 7:10–11).

Saint Paul refers in other passages to the relations between parents and children (Eph 6:1–4; Col 3:20–21; 1 Tim 3:4–5, 12; Tit 2:4–5).

The First Letter of Saint Peter also contains an extensive paragraph on marriage (see 1 Pet 3:1–7).

The last book of the New Testament, the Revelation to Saint John, portrays the Church in heaven by means of a nuptial image: "And I saw the holy city, new Jerusalem, coming down out of heaven from God, prepared as a bride adorned for her husband; and I heard a great voice from the throne saying, 'Behold, the dwelling of God is with men. He will dwell with them, and they shall be his people, and God himself will be with them'" (Rev 21:2–3). This passage suggests that the Church, the Spouse of Christ, is the place where God dwells with men. It is permissible to project this reality onto marriage, since in marriage this union is represented: *the Christian home must be a dwelling for God, a place of encounter with him*. Perhaps this is the passage that provides the basis for calling the Christian home "*the domestic Church*".

Saint Paul's teaching on marriage expresses, on the one hand, a very lofty spiritual ideal but, on the other hand, emphasizes very practical and concrete situations. This is only natural, since there is a tension in Christian life between the ideal of perfection, which is possible by virtue of God's grace, and human frailty, which bears the imprint and the consequences of sin.

Celibacy

While it is certainly true that there are texts in the Old Testament that attach religious importance to continence and attribute a special dignity to virginity (see Ex 19:15; Lev 15:18; 21:6–15; Ezek 44:22; 1 Sam 21:4–7), there was no such thing in Israel as consecration of oneself to God in the state of virginity. Only as the New Covenant approaches do the Gospels show us *John the Baptist*, a recluse in the desert, poor and austere, without a wife and without a home. It is no mere coincidence that he, living in the purity of celibacy, had the courage (which others did not have) to defend the purity of marriage and fidelity and to die for this cause.

Even more significant is the fact that the *Son of God* took human nature in the womb of a virgin woman who conceived him by power of the Holy Spirit and without the natural cooperation of a man (see Mt 1:18–25; Lk 1:26–38). The *virginity of Mary* was not merely a fortuitous circumstance, but rather the result of her deliberate intention, as we may infer from the question that she asked the angel who announced to her the incarnation of the Son of God in her womb: "How shall this be since I know not man?" (Lk 1:34 Greek, Vulgate, Douay-Rheims). The expression "not to know man", in Old Testament usage, means not to have sexual relations (see, for example, Gen 4:1, 17, 25). The fact that Mary had been betrothed to Joseph implies that there was a mutual agreement in this regard.

Jesus did not marry. His life was totally consecrated to his mission. Not content merely to give an example by his life, however, he also explained the meaning that celibacy, or the renunciation of marriage, could have. When he reestablished the original law concerning the indissolubility of marriage (Mt 19:3–9), excluding all [possibility] of divorce, and characterizing as adultery the union of a divorced person with another, his disciples said to him:

> "If such is the case of a man with his wife, it is not expedient to marry." But he said to them, "Not all men can receive this precept, but only those to whom it is given. For there are eunuchs who have been so from birth, and there are eunuchs

who have been made eunuchs by men, and there are eunuchs who have made themselves eunuchs for the sake of the kingdom of heaven. He who is able to receive this, let him receive it" (Mt 19:10–12).

The disciples' way of thinking on this matter, as in others, was earthbound. Jesus gave them an answer that perhaps not all of them understood at the moment, although we do not know whether there was a divorced person among the disciples of Jesus. The reply that Jesus makes very clearly suggests three things:

— In the first place, that *a voluntary renunciation of marriage is possible*, apart from cases in which there is a physical impediment or incapacity;
— that this voluntary renunciation *can have a religious meaning* and be done "for the sake of the kingdom of heaven"; and
— that understanding the meaning of this renunciation *is a gift from God*, which is not given to all to carry out, but only to those to whom this gift is granted.

The Apostle Paul gives us to understand that he voluntarily practiced celibacy (1 Cor 7:7) and praised the voluntary renunciation of marriage, explaining that this makes a person more available to serve the Lord (1 Cor 7:32–35), provided that he or she has received from the Lord that gift of practicing continence (verse 7).

Christian celibacy does not originate in a contempt for sexuality, which is a work of God, nor in an attempt to belittle the dignity of marriage, which was established by God, nor in a selfishness that refuses to accept the responsibilities and sacrifices involved in married life and parenthood. Rather, it is the result of *a call from God*, of a "vocation" to live according to the example of Jesus Christ and of the Virgin Mary, setting aside something that is quite legitimate, such as marriage, in order to anticipate in this life, to some extent, the manner in which the saints in heaven will live (see Mt 22:30). Celibacy for the sake of the kingdom of heaven *makes present that which is everlasting*, whereas marriage bears the marks of transitory realities. Yet marriage is also a sign of what is most permanent in God's plan: his spousal love for his people, and from this perspective, above and beyond the life of conjugal intimacy, it *points also to that which will never pass away*.

In this and in the previous chapter, we have made a brief survey of the texts from Sacred Scripture that deal with marriage. These are only the most important ones; there are many others. *It is strongly recommended that you look up those that are cited here merely as references, and not to be content with reading only those that are reprinted in full.* A careful reading shows that, in her doctrine, the Church has done nothing more than arrange and systematize what the Bible teaches concerning human actions and situations common to all peoples.

IV. The Doctrine of the Catholic Church on Marriage

Progress

There is no doubt that the faithful, in following the teaching of Sacred Scripture and the Magisterium of the lawful pastors, bishops, and popes, have always had a clear idea of marriage, and that many have labored to live it sincerely and conscientiously. It is also certain that there have been believers who, yielding to temptation and to human weakness, have distanced themselves from this doctrine by their conduct. The Church has endeavored to encourage and support the former and to bring about the repentance and conversion of the latter through her prayer and her preaching, and most especially through the sacrament of penance [reconciliation].

But there have always been occasions in the life of the Church when, for various reasons, people have called into question or denied the principles of the faith and Catholic doctrine on marriage. This is worse than the sins of weakness, because those who commit them accept the fact that what they are doing is at odds with the gospel, whereas to doubt or to deny doctrine is to question the very teaching of the Church. Occasionally these doubts and denials stem from the desire to justify oneself and one's actions, thus confirming the statement with which the early twentieth-century French Catholic writer Paul Bourget concludes his novel *The Divorce*: "*When one does not live what he believes, he ends up believing what he lives.*"

Whether to refute errors or to clarify her teaching—which is always the foundation of the spiritual life—the Church has constantly proposed, through her Magisterium, her binding doctrine on marriage. The setting forth of this doctrine has been a long process and has taken various forms, according to the needs of different times and circumstances.

We can cite, as landmarks of this process, the ecumenical councils of Florence (1438–1445), Trent (1545–1563), and Vatican II (1962–1965); the encyclicals *Casti connubii* of Pope Pius XI (1930) and *Humanae vitae* of Paul VI (1968); the Synod of Bishops in 1980, and numerous documents published by bishops and bishops' conferences. Though not, strictly speaking, an act of the authentic Magisterium, which is exclusively the competence of the pope and bishops, a document on marriage that was published by the International Theological Commission in 1978, with the permission of Paul VI, is also important.

Here we will present in outline form the principal components of the Catholic doctrine concerning marriage.

Marriage Is a Sacrament

The mutual consent of the two parties contracting marriage constitutes a sacred sign, established by Jesus Christ, that *produces in the spouses a special grace: that of living a conjugal life in Christian charity, helping each other to grow spiritually, and to procreate and educate children, making them disciples of Christ and children of the Church*. Marital consent is, then, a *religious act*, by its very meaning as well as by its fruits of grace and holiness. The parties contracting marriage—who must be baptized or else there can be no sacramental marriage—must celebrate the sacrament of matrimony in the state of grace. If it should happen that they are not in the state of grace, the marriage will be valid but will not immediately produce its fruit of grace; this will be received later, when the spouses repent of their sins and are reconciled with God and the Church.

Marriage Requires the Consent of Both Parties

Marriage comes about through an act of will of the contracting parties. This act of will, or consent, *is absolutely irreplaceable*, and no human authority, civil or ecclesiastical, can dispense from it. The consent must be free and not forced, and consists of each contracting party offering to and receiving from the other the right to make use of their bodies in a way that is ordered to the marital act, the natural fruit of which is procreation. Marital consent is *perpetual and exclusive* and must be *manifested externally* in the form established by the Church.

Marriage Is Indissoluble

Once this consent between two baptized persons has been given, and sexual union has been accomplished in the normal way, the bond between the spouses *is perpetual*, that is to say, it *will last until the death of one of the spouses*. No human authority can dissolve the marital bond that exists between two baptized persons who have consummated their marriage; this cannot be done by civil authority, or even by the authority of the Church. Nothing that may occur *after* the marriage can affect its validity: not incurable illness, or lack of children, or the absence or disappearance of one spouse (provided that the missing spouse is not dead), not adultery or marital problems, however serious they may be.

In extreme cases, a separation of the spouses may eventually be necessary, but this separation *does not authorize either spouse to enter into another lawful union as long as the other spouse is alive*. Catholic doctrine rejects divorce *absolutely*. The spouse who separates continues to be married, and if he is joined to another person, he commits the mortal sin of adultery. Indissolubility is so intrinsic to marriage that not even the mutual agreement of the parties can put an end to it. And if a marriage is entered into "temporarily", or if indissolubility is made conditional, such a union would not be a marriage and would have no validity.

The Rights the Spouses Give and Grant Each Other Are Exclusive

Each spouse gives himself to the other, and *only* to the other. Whether at the time when the sacrament of matrimony is celebrated or at any time thereafter, neither spouse has the right to give marital affection to any person other than his spouse. If he should happen to do so, he would be staining himself with a sin of impurity, whether by desire or by a physical act, and this affection and, worse yet, any eventual sexual intimacy would be adulterous acts. *Lifelong* fidelity is a property of marriage that is as important as indissolubility. And if one spouse is unfaithful to the other—which is a grave sin—that infidelity does *not free the innocent spouse* of the duty to remain faithful to the guilty one.

The grace of marriage powerfully supports the fidelity of the spouses, but it is necessary that each one cooperate with this grace, by avoiding dangerous dispositions, by separating oneself from persons toward whom one begins to feel an ambiguous affection, and by fostering love and understanding with the other spouse. To the extent that it is possible, separations, even temporary ones, should be avoided, unless the couple is able to abstain, without danger, from conjugal life. It is better to lose a business or a promotion than to put fidelity at risk.

Marriage Is Ordered to Procreation

Nature itself has endowed sexual union with the power to engender life, and that is why children are one of the *essential reasons for and ends of marriage*. To exclude from matrimonial consent the procreation of children is to falsify marriage, and if this exclusion were absolute, the marriage would be, despite all appearances, null and without validity. This does not mean that persons who cannot have children cannot get married; provided that they are capable of normal physical union, their consent is not vitiated.

These persons can love each other sincerely, and the fact that they cannot beget children makes their intimacy no less legitimate. Their love, however, will have a painful emptiness, which will have to be supplemented with greater mutual love, with more understanding, and with a generous practice of charity toward others. Sometimes the adoption of a child will open to them new horizons of love and responsibility. Various legitimate reasons may make it necessary for a couple *to regulate voluntarily the number of children* that may come. The Church is not opposed to that but demands that this regulation *not be accomplished by violating nature through artificial means.*[1]

It Is the Mission of Parents to Educate Their Children in a Christian Manner

It would be inadequate to suppose that the mission of parents is reduced to bringing children into the world and caring only for their physical and material development. If God has entrusted to them the gift of children, it is so that they may give them a *complete education*, making them contributing members of society and sharers in the Christian vocation. This is the reason why Christian parents present their children to the Church as soon as possible, that they may receive from her the sacrament of baptism, which is the seed of Christian life. They do so out of the conviction that there is

---

[1] Paul VI pointed out in *Humanae vitae* that "every action which, either in anticipation of the conjugal act, or in its accomplishment, or in the development of its natural consequences, proposes, whether as an end or as a means, to render procreation impossible [no. 14]" is illicit. On the other hand, "If . . . there are serious motives to space out births, which derive from the physical or psychological conditions of husband and wife, or from external conditions, the Church teaches that it is then licit to take into account the natural rhythms immanent in the generative functions, for the use of marriage in the infecund periods only, and in this way to regulate birth without offending the moral principles which have been recalled earlier [no. 16]." This doctrine has been reiterated constantly by the subsequent Magisterium— ED.

nothing more precious for their children than to be incorporated into the people of God, which is the Church, and in the Church to receive salvation.

But it is not enough for parents to ask for baptism for their children. It will also be necessary for them to give an example of Christian and Catholic living, by their actions, by their way of life, and by their good judgment. If children see no consistency between what their parents claim to believe and how they conduct themselves, doubt and indifference will begin to set in. It is also the duty of parents to be *the first to evangelize their children*; their first apostolate is to communicate to their children a love for Jesus Christ and for his Church, to teach them with simplicity the mysteries of the faith, and to develop in them the habit of judging their own actions and events that occur, in the light of the gospel.

It is a serious error to leave children alone in a kind of religious indifference, so that they can decide, under the pretext of respect for their personalities and their freedom, whether or not they will adhere to the faith once they reach adolescence or the age of maturity. Faith is a gift from God, and *every human being is called to the Christian life*, which is the only path fully complying with God's designs.

To abandon a child to fend for himself, without gently guiding him along the path of faith, *is to expose him to the danger of never finding that path* and to deprive him of the riches and joys of the Christian life. The faith cannot be very strong in those parents who do not consider it their greatest privilege and joy to transmit the faith to their children.

Marriage Is a "Vocation" and a "State"

To say that marriage is a "vocation" means that it is a call from God to live the Christian life according to the demands and graces of the conjugal "state". In other words, marriage corresponds to the will of God that calls the majority of Christians to grow in faith, hope, and charity within the bosom of this sacramental union, which becomes for them the framework and the concrete setting for their generous response to the call to live in Christ, just as some are called to follow the path of celibacy or virginity.

Since matrimony is a vocation and a state, it must be affirmed and believed that marriage, contracted in the sight of God and sustained by the Word of God, the sacraments, and prayer, is a *true and authentic path to sanctity and Christian perfection.*

*Among Christians There Can Be
No Marriage That Is Lawful Unless It Is
at the Same Time Sacramental*

In Christ, the union of a man and a woman is either the sacrament of matrimony, or else it is not lawful. In the eyes of the Catholic faith, there is no possibility of a legitimate conjugal union between two baptized persons that is not simultaneously the sacrament of matrimony, endowed with all of its properties, goods, and ends.

A kind of "trial marriage" is not admissible. Cohabitation cannot be viewed as an honorable "first step" toward marriage, without the marriage existing from the start. So-called "civil marriage" *is not a true marriage for Catholics,* but simply a civil formality to guarantee the civil, legal, and patrimonial effects of the true marriage, which is sacramental.

The faithful cannot consider living together to be legitimate if theirs is only a civil union. If they only go through a civil wedding ceremony, while capable of contracting marriage through the sacrament of matrimony, and they live as husband and wife, they will be committing the sin of *fornication* or *concubinage* (cohabitation). And if they contract a civil marriage, while unable to enter a sacramental marriage (because at least one of them is already united sacramentally to another person, for example), then in God's sight this will be *concubinage* or *adultery*, even though such a situation may be "in order" in terms of human law.

In more than a few countries, legislation concerning civil marriage can be explained by the fact that these countries are not Christian, although sometimes this legislation was introduced with deliberate antireligious intent. But once civil marriage has been established, the Church insists that her children celebrate it *also*, not as though it replaces or could ever replace the sacrament, but only to secure its legal effects with regard to society.

It should be quite clear, then, that sexual union between a man and a woman either is accomplished within marriage, in which case it is wholesome and legitimate, and even meritorious in the eyes of God, or else it is accomplished outside of marriage, and then it is a sin and an offense against God.

The Church Has the Right to Legislate concerning Marriage

The sacraments, although they were instituted and established by Jesus Christ, were entrusted by him to his spouse, the Church. All sacraments are acts of divine worship, and so is matrimony, which *consecrates* the spouses in the state of Christian life that we have described. The worship of God is carried out in the Church, under her guardianship and ordinance. For this reason, the Church, through the authority of her lawful pastors, can and must pass *laws concerning marriage*. Naturally, those laws cannot contradict what God himself established, but they can specify requirements and establish impediments. Without going into great detail, let us recall that the Church, for many centuries now, has *determined the form* in which marital consent must be expressed in order to be valid. This consent must be manifested at least before a priest [or deacon; CIC can. 1108] with faculties to receive it in the name of the Church, and before two witnesses besides.

In exceptional cases the consent can be given before the priest only, or before two witnesses only. In general, the consent is expressed during the course of the matrimonial rite.

Let us recall, too, that the Church can establish, and has established, *impediments* to, or prohibitions against, contracting marriage. I am not referring here to those impediments which depend on the nature of marriage, for example, the incapacity to perform a normal sexual act, or certain degrees of very close kinship (between siblings, or between parents and children)—impediments over which the Church has no authority. We are speaking here, rather, about other impediments which the Church established, and from which she can dispense for serious reasons.

Among these impediments are: certain age limits, certain degrees of consanguinity (kinship) that are more or less proximate (for example, between cousins), the impediment that exists between the murderer of a spouse and the surviving spouse, the vow of chastity taken by members of religious institutes, diaconal or priestly ordination; there is also an impediment when one of the engaged couple is not baptized, or when one is Catholic and the other a baptized non-Catholic Christian, and so forth.

The authority of the Church extends also to her right to *pronounce as to the validity or nullity* of a marriage, that is to say [in the latter case], to declare that a union of two persons, in spite of appearances, was never a marriage. Once an ecclesiastical tribunal has pronounced the judgment of nullity, those who *only seemingly* were spouses, even if they had considered themselves in good faith to be such, are free to enter into marriage with another person, since the first union was not a true marriage.

The Church, in legislating on marriage, does not do so in order to place obstacles or to curtail unduly the freedom of her children, but rather in order to safeguard the sanctity, the stability, and the ends of the marital state. That is why her laws must be *respected, obeyed in conscience*, and regarded with profound *gratitude* as well.

Summary

The nine preceding sections, in which we have tried to sum up Catholic doctrine on marriage, are no more than an effort to present in an orderly way what Sacred Scripture says. We will now give a brief summary of this teaching.

Through baptism man is incorporated into the Church, is made a member of the Body of Christ, consecrates his life to God so as to honor him with his life and his worship, and takes on secular responsibilities as a task received from God, as a way of practicing charity and as a path leading to eternal life. Confirmation endows the Christian with the gift of the Holy Spirit and strengthens the grace of the apostolate. The Eucharist, the summit of the entire Christian life, unites the Church with the sacrifice of praise that Christ offers to the Father in heaven.

Matrimony is the sacrament that reflects the mystery of Christ's love for his Church. Christians join in matrimony above all to praise God and honor him through this sacrament, which is the broadest in terms of its meaning, just as baptism is the most necessary and the Eucharist is the most important because of its content. The law of marriage is none other than that which shines forth in the union of Christ with his Church. This union is *definitive, faithful, fruitful, holy,* and *sanctifying.* That is why marriage is *indissoluble, exclusive, ordered to the procreation and Christian education of children,* and *a state of life conducive to sanctity.*

Christians get married for God, and that is the best guarantee that their love will be safe from the vicissitudes of life and human frailties. They have children *for God,* in such a way that they may be not only citizens of this world, but also *people of faith who journey toward eternal life in the midst of and by means of their secular responsibilities.*

Faith and the Christian conscience see in the ordination of deacons, priests, and bishops and in religious vows, *a special consecration to God.* And so it is. But they should not fail to *regard marriage, also, as a consecration to God,* in order to serve him and to be sanctified in the marital state, through the lawful joys of love and of parenthood, and through the inevitable sacrifices that are the presence of the cross in the life of every disciple of Jesus Christ.

That is why we speak of the home as a "*domestic Church*", since it is a place of praise to God, of sanctification, of proclaiming the gospel to the children, a place of prayer and of practicing faith, hope, charity, and all the Christian virtues. The normal atmosphere of a Christian home is religious because, within it, *all are living for God, and from him they receive grace and holiness.* If a family lives in a home in this way, it will be no surprise if God blesses it by calling one of its children to his holy service in the priestly ministry or in religious life; and parents should consider this vocation as a distinct honor and as the most precious fruit of their love for one another in God.

V. Preparation for Marriage

Remote (Long-term) Preparation

What has been said thus far about matrimony clearly demonstrates the great dignity of this sacrament and the serious responsibilities that those who contract marriage take upon themselves. The basic requirement for those who wish to marry is the possession of a *human and Christian maturity* that will serve as the foundation for such a noble state of Christian life. It would be a grave error to think, because marriage is a sacrament which communicates the grace of God, that grace will compensate for any deficiency, as if the sacraments did not require man's cooperation to bring about their salvific effects.

It is almost impossible to determine all the elements that constitute an adequate maturity, which is capable of making marriage a responsible and not a reckless act.

Let us start by considering some aspects that we could call *human*.

The first one might well be *earnestness*, which is the opposite of frivolity or superficiality. It involves having a balanced and responsible outlook on life, capable of delving into the deeper meaning of things and not remaining at the level of appearances.

Next would come, almost as a consequence, *discipline*. This means the ability to resist being carried away by the impulses of the moment, knowing instead how to set goals and to determine means to attain them, vigorously persevering in the efforts to achieve them. Discipline presupposes the will power necessary to carry out a resolution at some cost, as well as to set aside what might be pleasurable, but not really beneficial, or that which is even harmful.

Next we could point to *industriousness* or diligence, an important quality, since in a home serious work is demanded of both the husband and the wife. It is rather likely that a lazy person will end up neglecting important obligations in marriage.

Tolerance, adaptability, and *respect* in dealing with others are character traits that are undeniably important for family life. Conversely, rigidity, high-handedness, and a domineering attitude do not serve to build and maintain harmonious relations.

Mastery over one's own *character*, especially in people prone to anger or bouts of rage, is an essential prerequisite for living together in the future.

Sincerity and *loyalty* are indispensable factors in civil life and in marital life as well. The inability to admit one's own mistakes causes friction and, once that occurs, makes matters worse.

The ability to *forgive* and to *forget* the offenses and mistakes of others also plays an important role.

The *strength* to face setbacks without becoming discouraged, and not to spend one's life lamenting what might have been and never was, is a distinctive mark of human maturity that is necessary in life and in marriage.

The *humility* to accept not always being on center stage, and to recognize one's own limitations and the strengths and qualities of others, is a disposition that promotes interaction with other people and makes *patience* possible.

Justice makes us understand that we all have duties and rights, and it prevents that self-centered attitude of thinking that we alone have rights, whereas everybody else has duties only. We are inclined, however, to forget our duties as well as the rights of others.

Generosity is also opposed to selfishness. It manifests itself in many ways, from an attitude of detachment with respect to material goods to the willingness to please and to comply with the legitimate likes and dislikes of others, even at the cost of renunciation and sacrifice.

Discretion respects the realm of our intimacy and that of others. Frequently, mistakes are taken more seriously than they deserve, and it is more difficult to put them right, simply because of indiscreet and exaggerated remarks.

Of utmost importance is *chastity*, or *purity*. It is a fact known from experience that the sexual urge can easily go astray and is not always easy to control. Chastity is the virtue that moderates and sets limits to this urge. Purity refers not only to external acts but also to thoughts and words, and only within an atmosphere of purity is a truly decent relationship possible between men and women.

There are times when the development of a person's maturity is affected not by occasional or persistent character flaws (this occurs in all of us), but rather (what is in a certain sense more serious) by psychological imbalances that can exceed the bounds of normal behavior. It is important to detect them and to seek the advice of a competent professional who can help correct them.

Although the traits and virtues listed above are usually called "human", it is no less true that they form an integral part of the Christian life, in which they should grow and develop as an adequate response to the ideal of man, who was made in the image of God and whose perfect realization and model is Jesus Christ.

But a Christian marriage is founded also—and this is extremely important—on elements that are *explicitly* Christian.

The first of them all is *faith*, that is, a steadfast adherence to what God has taught us through his Word, which is handed on to us by the Church. "Faith is the assurance of things hoped for, the conviction of things not seen" (Heb 11:1). Faith is the gift from God that opens us to an understanding of the deepest meaning of human life. It is like a powerful light that allows us to see and comprehend what is not perceptible to human intelligence left to its own devices.

Faith is joined by *hope*, which is trust in God's faithfulness and in the fulfillment of his promises, in this life and in the life to come.

Charity, by which we love God for who he is and our fellow men because they are God's work, his children, is the root and perfection of the Christian life. It could not be otherwise because "God is love, and he who abides in love abides in God, and God abides in him" (1 Jn 4:16).

Saint Paul says that charity "binds everything together in perfect harmony" (Col 3:14) as though he wanted to compare it with a cord that keeps a bundle neatly wrapped up, if you will pardon the expression. The same Apostle wrote an admirable passage in which he exalts the magnificence of charity (see 1 Cor 13:1–13).

If matrimony is a sacrament, the profound meaning of which is discovered only in the light of faith, and if it is a path to holiness, the root and expression of which is charity, it is quite obvious that these virtues are an essential prerequisite for embarking on a married life that is in keeping with the Christian ideal.

But there is more. The life of a Christian necessarily has its meaning in rendering worship to God. This worship has two aspects that are intimately connected: life itself (see Rom 12:1–2) and the liturgy of the Church, which was established by Jesus Christ and is carried out principally in the sacraments. The *sacramental life*, then, is an essential element of Christian and Catholic life.

Attendance at Mass on Sundays, and even on other days of

the week, receiving the Body of Christ in Holy Communion, and having recourse to the sacrament of penance to confess our sins: all these are elements that take on special significance in the perspective of matrimony. And since marriage will make new spiritual and apostolic demands, it stands to reason that couples enter into it after having received the gift of the Holy Spirit in the sacrament of confirmation.

A *life of prayer* is also important. Reflecting on the words of Christ, on his example, and on his saving acts is a source of spiritual perspective upon every aspect of life. Turning to God to ask him for what we need, and precisely in the order of the intentions expressed in the Our Father (Mt 6:9–13), is a necessity for someone who knows that he is a poor sinner, in need of rectifying continually the impulses of his heart and of receiving from God what only he can give us. It is obvious that no one can claim to possess perfectly all that is necessary to enter into marriage. Still, it is good to be aware of the ideal and to pursue it with confidence. The man and the woman who are thinking of getting married some day must examine themselves as to the state of their long-term preparation; they should also determine, with objectivity and without being blinded by their feelings, whether the person on whom they have set their sights, as a possible companion in life, fulfills, at least adequately, the conditions for making a home according to Christian principles and ideals.

When we see, with sorrow, that a marriage is failing, we need to ask how this lamentable situation came to pass. Most times, not to say always, it becomes clear that there were failings well before the marriage ceremony took place, problems that were not resolved at the time and that, with the passing of years, far from all spiritual life, progressively worsened and eventually caused the breakdown.

A young Christian man or woman contemplating the prospect of being married some day must realize that preparation for this state of life is insufficient if it is carried out only in the courtship phase, during the engagement, or while attending a few premarital talks. Instead, they must be well-grounded in a *formation* that starts in childhood, develops in adolescence and youth, and coalesces in maturity.

Proximate (Short-term) Preparation

This stage comprises what we call "courtship" and, following that, formal engagement.

Courtship consists in an affectionate relationship within the perspective of a *possible* marriage. It is not, strictly speaking, an engagement, but rather a period in which mutual interaction allows the young people to discover whether they are really meant for each other, whether they share the same ideals and are capable of adapting. A Christian courtship should *never* be merely a form of recreation, a pastime, or a sort of game played with the emotions.

No general rule can be established as to how long it should last, but neither extreme is advisable; a courtship can be too long or excessively brief, and each one has its disadvantages. People who are dating have not entered into a formal engagement, so there is nothing blameworthy about it if they decide to end their relationship, whether by mutual agreement or because one of them decides to do so, even if this causes suffering for the other.

Courtship, above all in its initial stages, is a *"trial" situation*, in which there is room for doubts and uncertainties, which will eventually have to be resolved definitively, positively or negatively. Since courtship is something *serious*, it must take the future into consideration and prepare for it. A courtship that interferes seriously, or even not so seriously, with study or with work, lacks the quality of responsibility and true respect for oneself and for the other; love is more and demands more than beautiful feelings.

Basically, courtship is a stage during which preparations are made for the definitive choice. It is characterized by ever-deepening emotions, but it is necessary that these feelings, however powerful and absorbing they may be, leave sufficient *freedom* to reflect on present and future realities and not lead to getting carried away by romantic illusions.

It is clear that the *final decision as to marriage* is something that belongs solely to the couple who plan to contract it. However, one should not underestimate the sound judgment of impartial persons concerning the man or the woman who is courting. Of particular importance is the judgment of the parents, whose intuitions about the future companions of their children are usually more clear-sighted than might appear at first.

As in all aspects of Christian life, prayer must accompany the entire time of courtship. It is essential to ask God fervently to grant to each one the light needed to discern both one's own good qualities and shortcomings and those of the other and not to exaggerate or undervalue either of them.

One must humbly pray that the ordinary Christian vision of life be preserved and grow during courtship, a theme that from many angles ought to be a subject of conversation and discussion. And since affection tends to express itself physically, one must also pray that the Lord will preserve this time of courtship in a spirit of Christian purity and chastity. On this point, let no one presume upon his own strength or that of the other; it is necessary to have the courage to avoid occasions or situations that place purity in danger, causing the best intentions to end in disaster.

The *engagement* goes one step further. By various means, and according to different customs and family traditions, it starts as a public commitment to enter into marriage within a reasonable period of time. Sometimes this commitment is expressed by exchanging and wearing rings, which are usually blessed by a priest or a deacon.

Occasionally, the groom's parents will make a formal visit to the parents of the bride and "ask" them for their daughter on behalf of their son, thus demonstrating that they are in agreement with the young man's decision. In other cases, there is a family gathering at which the engagement is formalized. It is usual for the engagement to precede marriage by only a little while, a few months at most.

In taking this step and making this commitment, it is assumed that the affection between the two future spouses has matured sufficiently so as to *dissipate doubts* and uncertainties, inasmuch as that is humanly possible, about their forthcoming and final decision to contract marriage. But it is clear that the engagement is not of an irrevocable nature, as marriage is, and thus one cannot view the breaking of an engagement as something inappropriate, whether it be by the will of both parties or of only one.

Nevertheless, it stands to reason that these breaks are not frequent, and if they occur there must be serious reasons for them. In any case, it is a thousand times *better to break an engagement than to run the risk of an unhappy marriage*. If the engaged couple have reached the conclusion that they will not be able to form a lifelong union, no social convention or personal convenience should prevent them from breaking off a commitment that, instead of a bond of love, has become a prospect of painful slavery.

There is one word that applies as much to courtship as it does to engagement and marriage: we say that this man and this woman form "a couple". Naturally, this word does not have exactly the same meaning in each of these three stages, but it does nonetheless have something in common. "Couple" means two things that are similar, homogeneous, without notable differences. In the case of a man and a woman, being "a couple" implies that there are *shared interests and a common vision of life, without any significant cultural, social, intellectual, or spiritual disparities.*

It is true that one of the fruits of conjugal life is an increasing communality of life and interests, but it is no less certain that a couple runs a very serious risk when there are *considerable differences between the two at the outset*, because experience proves that differences which are too pronounced and evident are difficult to overcome. God works miracles, but he is not obliged to work them in order to solve problems caused by the imprudence and rash decisions of men.

By the eve of the wedding, the Christian engaged couple should have learned to love each other in Christ, to accept each other and the immediate family of the other, to pray together, and to renounce, for the sake of harmony, even one's own legitimate wishes and preferences.

We must add a few comments on a very delicate subject: that of a love between two persons when *one is a Catholic and the other professes another religion.* This is a serious difference that can affect the couple's shared vision of life, as well as their moral criteria with respect to various situations, to the doctrine about marriage itself, and to the education of their children. These are so-called "*mixed marriages*". The extent of these differences can vary a great deal. It is smaller if both are Christian, even though one of them is Orthodox, Anglican, or Protestant rather than Catholic. It is much greater if one of the parties is not a Christian but, for example, Jewish, Muslim, or pagan. And the same is true when one of the parties, although baptized, has completely lost the faith.

The Church *advises against* such marriages, because in them *one of the most important elements* that form the basis of a common life *will be missing*, namely: *unity in faith and in religious convictions*. Frequently such marriages drift into religious indifference or coolness in both spouses and give rise to painful tension about how the children should be educated. When two people are in love, especially if their religious convictions are not very firm or deep, they tend to underestimate the difficulties that arise from a mixed marriage and usually do not understand the weighty reasons, borne out by experience, which move the Church, for the good of her children, to dissuade them from a marriage influenced by this fundamental difference.

In order to avoid greater evils, the bishop or his vicar will usually dispense them from the matrimonial impediment, established in Church law, which prohibits mixed marriages. Once the dispensation is granted, the engaged couple can contract marriage, but this dispensation is no guarantee that this union will be completely successful. When the dispensation is requested, the Catholic party must make a commitment to raise all of his children in the Catholic faith, and he must inform his future spouse of this obligation, so that misunderstandings do not crop up later.

If the mixed marriage is contracted *between two baptized persons*, it will be a *sacramental marriage for both*, and this is so even if the non-Catholic party belongs to a Christian community (and there are many) which does not acknowledge that marriage has the dignity of a sacrament. But if the non-Catholic party is not baptized, then the *matrimonial bond* that comes about between them will be *natural and not sacramental*, because the basis for sacramentality is the representation of the union of Christ with his Church, and this presupposes that *both* contracting parties have been incorporated through baptism into the Body of Christ, which is his Church. This type of marriage, legitimate but not sacramental, does not have the characteristic of indissolubility in the same degree that a sacramental marriage does.

Immediate Preparation

Since a Catholic marriage must be celebrated before the Church, once the engaged couple have decided on a date for their sacramental union, it will be necessary to make some immediate preparations.

The first is the "*matrimonial investigation*". This is carried out in the parish, usually that of the bride, in the presence of the parish priest or his delegate. It consists of a questionnaire to be filled out with information about each of the future spouses. A *recently issued* baptismal certificate for each of them must be presented, and it must be determined whether or not they have received the sacrament of confirmation.

The purpose of the "investigation" is to place on record the fact that the engaged couple *intend* to contract marriage according to the teaching of the Church and, similarly, that they are *free* to enter into marriage, that is to say, that they are not joined in sacramental matrimony to any other person and that there are no *impediments* to their contracting marriage with one another, in conformity with ecclesiastical law.

If, during the course of the investigation, some impediment appears from which the Church can dispense, the pastor will have recourse to the competent authority, usually the Ordinary, to apply for it. It could happen that one of the parties is *married, but only civilly, to another person*. If he is Catholic, that marriage is not valid before God or the Church, because for a Catholic there is no valid marriage other than sacramental marriage. This person is able to marry in Church, but because this creates a situation with legal complications, which may even be punishable under civil law, his eventual sacramental marriage to a person other than the one to whom he is wedded civilly, must be *authorized by the Ordinary*.

The matrimonial investigation concludes with declarations by two witnesses who can either be relatives or friends of the engaged couple. It requires also the parents' consent if one of the parties is *underage* before the law.

In many dioceses, bishops have decreed that the engaged couple must participate, before entering into marriage, in a series of preparatory *talks*. The purpose of these talks is to remind them about the Church's teaching on Christian marriage. It would be a delusion to think that a few talks could provide everything that is contained in what we have called "long-term" and "short-term" preparation, yet they are useful and can be the point of departure for an effort to re-encounter the Christian meaning of life and of marriage.

The "immediate preparation" must be made at an opportune time, at least two months prior to the date selected for the wedding.

VI. The Rite of the Sacrament of Matrimony

In the early days of Christianity, Christians complied with popular practices and customs when entering into marriage, while at the same time purifying those customs of everything that was foreign to the Christian meaning and spirit of the ceremony.

As time went on, the consent of the contracting parties, a fundamental and irreplaceable element of marriage, was given and ratified within the framework of a liturgical celebration. In the East, more importance was given to the intervention of the priest, whereas in the West, even though the presence of a priest or deacon is generally required, more emphasis has been placed upon the role of the contracting parties. In Western theology it is usually stated that the parties to the marriage are the *ministers of the sacrament of matrimony*; this expression means that the manifestation of their will is absolutely necessary, and that from it springs the sacred bond, together with the graces of the marital state.

The norm, liturgically and doctrinally speaking, is that *marriage takes place during the celebration of Mass, or the Holy Eucharist.* The reason is quite clear: matrimony is a sacrament that *consecrates* Christians in the state of conjugal life in which the couple *offer their lives to God* so as to express the mystery of Christ's love for his Church through their own spousal love and in order to increase the people of God with new children.

This consecration is situated within the Christian vocation, which is nothing else than *living for God.* And this consecration is expressed *in the Mass or the Eucharist,* in which *the faithful and the whole Church are incorporated into the offering that Christ made and makes of himself to the Father,* an offering that is made present in the celebration of the Eucharistic Sacrifice. When we look at things this way, and there is no other way to look at them if one has faith, the celebration of matrimony is *a religious act, an act of divine worship, a consecration to holiness, and the most fitting occasion for it, therefore, is Holy Mass.*

The wedding Mass retains the structure of any other celebration of the Eucharist, with some adaptations. Of course, except in cases when this celebration takes place on a very important feast day, the biblical readings will refer to matrimony, and there are several to choose from, which is usually done in accordance with the couple's wishes. After the Gospel reading and the homily, the priest asks for the consent of the contracting parties. There are various formulas for expressing it. In the most common one, the priest asks each of them: *N., do you take N. to be your wife [husband]? Do you promise to be true to her [him] in good times and in bad, in sickness and in health, to love her [him] and honor her [him] all the days of your life?* To which the other responds aloud: *I do.*

The priest or the deacon then blesses those who have just become husband and wife, and they proceed to the blessing and exchange of rings, which are the symbol of the marital state and of faithfulness in love.

The Mass continues with the general intercessions, which in this case contain special prayers for the newlyweds. There is also a proper Preface for the wedding Mass, and special petitions for the spouses are even interpolated in the Canon, or "great Eucharist Prayer".

After the Our Father, the priest gives the newlyweds the solemn nuptial blessing.

The couple receive Holy Communion under both species of bread and wine, if they wish.

At the conclusion of the Mass, there is a special final blessing for the spouses as well.

When, for serious reasons, a wedding does not take place during the celebration of Holy Mass, the structure of the rite is similar: there are biblical readings, the manifestation of consent, the blessing of the rings, general intercessions, a solemn nuptial blessing, and the final blessing. Holy Communion can also be given to the spouses.

In remote places where there is no priest, or in parishes in which, due to a clergy shortage, there is no resident priest, the bishop can authorize a layman to preside over marriages, acting as an official witness of the Church. And it can happen, in special cases and in far-removed places, that a Catholic sacramental marriage can be contracted in the presence of two witnesses only. A marriage thus contracted is perfectly valid, since the essential element is accomplished, namely, the consent of contracting parties.

In every marriage, except in cases of emergency or in danger of death, it is necessary that there be at least two witnesses to listen to the manifestation of consent. These witnesses are usually called the "best man" and the "maid (or matron) of honor"; they must be respectable people who, by their Christian life, will be an example for the newlyweds. It is wrong to choose as witnesses persons whose lives are not expressions of Christian faith and morality. But if such persons are chosen, that does not invalidate the marriage.

From all we have said so far, it should be clear that the celebration of marriage is *an act of divine worship, a religious act, and a moment of intense prayer for the couple and for their future home.* Unfortunately, this sacramental act frequently takes the form of a social event in which outward trappings are emphasized more than its essential character as an act of worship, as if a church wedding were nothing more than carrying out a traditional formality. That is why some people have misgivings about how long the ceremony will take—they act as though they were in a hurry to get it over with as soon as possible!

It is sad to see that many people attend weddings merely to fulfill some social obligation, without any spirit of prayer whatsoever, more worried about checking to see who is in attendance and who is not and about what this or that guest is wearing. It would be better if fewer people attended, if those who are in such a hurry would stay at home or do whatever they have to do, and if those who do attend would do so in a spirit of prayer for the couple who are about to found a home together, participating in Holy Mass and receiving Holy Communion during the celebration of the sacrament.

There is a prayer in the liturgical rite of the celebration of matrimony that summarizes with admirable concision the Catholic teaching about this sacrament:

> Father, keep them always true to your commandments.
> Keep them faithful in marriage
>   and let them be living examples of Christian life.
> Give them the strength which comes from the gospel
>   so that they may be witnesses of Christ to others.
> Bless them with children
>   and help them to be good parents.
> May they live to see their children's children.
> And, after a happy old age,
>   grant them fullness of life with the saints
>   in the kingdom of heaven.
> We ask this through Christ our Lord. Amen.

Of course, nothing stands in the way, once the wedding ceremony has taken place, of celebrating the event with joyful, Christian family festivities. Jesus himself attended a wedding feast (see John 2:1–11) and, so that nothing would spoil the happiness of the bride and groom, he performed on that occasion his first miracle, changing water into wine.

VII. The Virtue of Chastity, or Purity [2]

General Remarks

We have already said that, as a result of sin, the attraction between man and woman and the sexual drive no longer possess the harmony and delicacy that God intended and that existed in the beginning. So the realm of sexuality is marked by attitudes of curiosity, slyness, and selfishness that must be controlled and rectified.

Men are commonly prone to look at women as objects to satisfy their sensual and genital urges, and even those who sincerely strive to live according to the gospel of Jesus Christ feel impulses arise, prior to any reflection, that are not upright. Men are able to disassociate the desire for the body of a woman from true love.

Some men, in fact, consider "success" with women, "adventures", and "escapades" as authentic and normal expressions of their virility. Consequently, they think of woman as a "trophy" that one gains or collects, almost as an unavoidable necessity. Indeed, it would appear to some as a defect in their manhood not to "take advantage" of an occasion to have sex with a woman. When things are viewed from a Christian perspective, such behavior is not far from that of animals, and is even worse, because animals do not mate outside of the fertile period.

The sexuality of a woman differs from that of a man: it is less violent and more dependent upon affection. A woman does not immediately feel the same urge toward the body of man that a man experiences toward her body. But many times, without fully realizing how provocative she is being,

[2] A more extensive treatment of this subject is found in the essay "On Chastity", reprinted as part two, chapter five of this book.— ED.

she easily strikes strongly suggestive poses that provoke in the male reactions that then surprise her. The woman cannot imagine the extent to which showing off her figure can represent for a man an incentive that impels him toward what is not precisely for the best. Some women engage in an ambiguous and very often unconscious game of provocation and prudery, imagining the limits to be far beyond what they allow themselves, when in reality they are amply exceeding those boundaries—and then they complain about the consequences.

In terms of Catholic morality, the sexual union of a man and a woman who are not husband and wife constitutes the sin of *fornication* when both are single. It is a grave sin and an abuse of sexuality; the fact that it took place by mutual agreement is no excuse. If the man has forced the woman, the sin is one of *violation* and is still more grave. If the violated woman is underage, the sin is compounded with additional malice. If one or both persons in a sexual union have a legitimate spouse, the sin is extremely serious and is called *adultery*. We are not going to enumerate kinds of sexual abuse that are perhaps less frequent. But it is necessary to mention *masturbation*, which consists in procuring sexual pleasure with oneself.

All abusive sexual behavior has an element in common: it seeks outside of marriage a satisfaction that God has decreed to be something proper to marriage. Physical union between a man and a woman is an act that has a meaning that, if it were expressed in words, would be as follows: "I am giving myself to you until death, and you to me; I assume total responsibility for you, physically and spiritually, forever, and you for me; and we both assume responsibility for our children, the fruit of our love." That is what a sexual act signifies, and if there is no marriage, that meaning is absent.

What has just been said may strike some people as strange

or surprising; various comparisons can help make it comprehensible. A sexual act outside marriage is like a gearbox outside an automobile: something without a meaning and a purpose of its own. Or like a check that bounces, which in outward appearance is the same as a check drawn on an account with sufficient funds; it is supposed to mean something, but in reality it does not, since the thing signified does not exist. Or like a typical bottle with a label indicating high-quality contents, except that in reality it does not contain what the label says, whether perfume, liquor, or medicine.

This is why sexual union outside of marriage contains a deplorable element of falsehood and lying, because the lies are not always in the words, but are quite frequently in the deeds. There is, furthermore, a mockery of nature and of God's law, and also, though it may not be considered as such, a mockery of oneself and of the other.

Adultery is even more serious. It contains *three different kinds of abuse* in one and the same act. The first is the one already described in the preceding paragraph. The second is the outrageous disregard for the exclusive right of the other spouse, a disregard and abuse that is all the more disloyal inasmuch as the adulterer would usually be indignant if he were to find himself deceived by the spouse whom he himself has been deceiving. There is, therefore, a manifest injustice, which is not excusable even by the "permission" of the spouse, which no married person can give according to the law of God. The third abuse is the offense to the sacrament itself, that is, an attack on matrimony insofar as it is the sign and representation of the love of Christ for his Church. Hence, adultery is an offense against three virtues: *chastity*, *justice*, and *religion*.

Fornication and adultery are external sins in which the sexual act is consummated outside the order established by God. There are other external sins against purity. We have already mentioned *masturbation*, in which there is an element of selfishness. It usually appears in adolescence, and it is more common in boys than in girls. It can easily turn into a habit that is difficult to eradicate. In women, it is often dependent upon psychological factors, such as feelings of loneliness, pessimism, and depression.

There are also other external sins against purity, such as *petting* and *sexual glances*. Internal sins against chastity are sexual thoughts and desires, to the extent that one *voluntarily and deliberately consents to them*. Thoughts that are rejected as soon as one becomes aware that they are not in conformity with the law of God are not sins, nor are desires, however vehement they may be, if they are not accepted and one struggles to overcome them. The best way to do away with impure thoughts or desires is to direct our attention to other things, offering a quick prayer to God that he may give us the strength not to turn away from him.

Nowadays, powerful inducements to impurity exist, arising from a veritable *commercialization of sex*. The utilization of the feminine figure as the subject of all sorts of advertising and, still worse, pornographic magazines and films, are tools for demolishing the healthy atmosphere of purity that ought to exist. Many times without realizing it, our sisters—grown women—*dress* in such a way that they do not exactly provoke thoughts and feelings that are pure. A Christian woman ought to reflect on her responsibility not to provoke in men those urges that distance them from God and from Christian holiness. The unwholesome desire to be admired at all costs makes some women become accomplices to sins of thought and desire, for which they will have to answer before God, because their provocation is a sin against charity.

Another inducement to impurity is created by the custom of making sex the subject of *risqué conversations*, as though something that was destined by God to have such a noble purpose, which is fulfilled in marriage, could be mere entertainment, a pastime, or an occasion for vanity.

In the difficult task of keeping oneself within the bounds of Christian conduct in the area of sexuality, *modesty* plays a very important role. There are some who believe that modesty is a kind of prudishness, a psychological complex, an inability to be "natural", or even something abnormal. This attitude stems from the error of ignoring the fact that human nature was vitiated by sin and that not every urge is in and of itself healthy and right. On the contrary, Christian modesty is a form of respect and reserve in an area where, as we know very well, excesses are easy.

Purity during Courtship and Engagement

The growing affection between a man and a woman [during the stages of courtship and engagement] necessarily poses the problem of controlling sexual impulses. This is because affection, however sound and well-intentioned it may be, tends to express itself in forms that gradually acquire sensual overtones. This affection can obscure, between those who love each other, the boundaries of what is correct.

Many people excuse their impure conduct by saying that "it was for love". Human affection necessarily has a spiritual dimension and a physical element, but it is absolutely essential that the physical element be controlled by the spiritual aspect, or else it falsifies and injures true love.

We have to keep in mind that being in love diminishes resistance to that which is improper except within marriage, and for that reason, dating and the engagement are situations in which, if they are to be a Christian experience, one must reinforce one's vigilance, self-control, and prayer.

The first condition for keeping a Christian love within due limits before marriage is the presence of a *profound conviction* that purity is an important virtue in the life of every disciple of Jesus Christ. Recalling that *the body is a "temple of the Holy Spirit"* (see I Cor 3:16–17; 6:19; 2 Cor 6:16) is a great help in resisting disordered sexual impulses.

Respect for the living temple of God, which we are, is something that must be shown in one's own attitude and in that of the other. To sin against purity with the human being whom we love is to harm him in his relationship with God, and that injury can never go by the sacred name of love. For the same reason, it is wrong to call an unchaste act "a proof of love".

The second condition is to *avoid dangerous situations*. Experience proves that human frailty runs significant risks in situations where external circumstances favor disorder. This is true in any department of life, and that is why it is a sin, not only to commit a reproachable act, but also to *put oneself needlessly into situations that are known to facilitate or very often to lead to something that should not happen.*

For those who are in steady relationships or engaged to be married, some situations are particularly risky: being together away from other people for prolonged periods; conversations that drift toward titillating subjects; lack of modesty in one's posture and gestures; excessive physical proximity; prolonged caresses, especially if they lead to touching parts of the body that are highly excitable to oneself or to the other; alcoholic drinks, which diminish the vigilance of the conscience; worse yet, certain stimulating drinks, and so forth.

Each one must be attentive so as not to be a cause of sin for the other. Precisely for the sake of Christian love, each one must put a quick and decisive stop to whatever might lead, in oneself or in the other, to offending God. There are couples who think that if they do not go all the way and have sexual relations, then the rest is of no great importance and would be, at most, a venial sin. That is not so. Any deliberate search for or any voluntary acceptance of sexual pleasure, any position that by itself causes serious arousal, is a grave sin before God. There is no sin, however, in desires or thoughts that are promptly rejected, which arise from a healthy and delicate expression of affection.

The third condition is an intense spiritual life. If courtship and engagement aspire to that life in common which is marriage, which represents the sacred union that exists between Christ and the Church, it is natural that they develop in an atmosphere of spirituality and of seeking God, that they be, so to speak, a token of what will one day be marital sanctity.

That is why a Christian couple in love will assign *great importance to the sacramental life*, frequently receiving the *Eucharist and the sacrament of penance, praying together* to the Lord and to the Virgin Mary, so that their love may not be merely a human sentiment but a manifestation of their life in Christ.

Of special importance is frankness and openness with one's confessor, so as to receive from him not only the forgiveness of sins but help and advice for living love in a Christian manner. And if there should be weaknesses and falls, the grace of the sacrament of penance will help in starting anew, in correcting the course, and in avoiding what experience has shown to be wayward and harmful.

Purity in the courtship and the engagement not only is important for the *present* spiritual life of those who love each other, but also is *a good preparation* for marriage.

Of course, a love that is pure means that when the time comes to marry, the consent will be *freer*, motivated solely by love. When love has not been pure, bonds of dependence arise that create *feelings of obligation*, something that is not healthy or advantageous for matrimonial consent. If the couple's conduct has not been chaste, it can happen that, in a moment of vacillation about whether to end the relationship or the engagement for good reasons, it is not ended because there are carnal "ties" that make the couple fear breaking it off, which nevertheless would be the best thing to do.

Impurity during the courtship or engagement can lead later on, during marriage and in moments of crisis or difficulties, to the voicing of the reproach or the excuse: "I married because I had to."

Worse still is the situation in which, as a result of premarital sexual relations, a child is conceived. Frequently such a baby is considered a lamentable accident or even a curse. If the couple's moral consciences are degraded, they will think of having an *abortion*, which makes the only one who was innocent in the whole affair pay with his life, while the couple *stain their hands with the blood of a child*. What in marriage would have been seen as a blessing from God is regarded as a calamity.

In other cases, and often due to family pressure, a "quick marriage" seems to be the only way out of the situation. It can happen that this may be justified, but it is not without its risks, especially if the child on the way constitutes a constraining factor. If previously there was no mature and profound love, the most advisable thing would be to have the child while unmarried and to marry later, or not at all, thus avoiding the immense risk of being forced by this circumstance into a marriage that would be, not a community of love, but rather a chain of slavery.

Those who have begotten a child and do not get married because they did not really love each other are more worthy of respect than those who, out of *pride, vanity,* or *hypocrisy,* hide their sin with a *crime, fearing to face up to their responsibility.*

In any case, it is clear that, if there is not genuine and responsible love, the fact of having begotten a child does not constitute a moral obligation to enter into marriage.

But chastity during courtship and engagement becomes *important, also, later on* in marital life. For a wide variety of reasons it will happen that, when one or both of the spouses desire physical union, it will not always be possible. Whether because one of them is very tired or indisposed, or because of illness or a lack of suitable privacy; whether because obligations of various sorts require the absence of one of the spouses, or out of respect at a time of bereavement or other adversities; whether, finally, because of a need to space out or regulate childbearing, it will be necessary to abstain from the sexual act.

In such cases, the *self-control* acquired during a pure youth and a chaste engagement will be a great help, because the virtues and Christian conduct cannot be improvised, but must be practiced and learned.

Chastity in Marriage

In marriage, sexual union between the spouses is a *very important expression of love and the means of fruitfulness chosen by God.* Here, this union is "a true union", that is to say, it is a sign of the union of Christ with his Church, expressing a mutual self-giving that is faithful and loving and sealed by the sacrament until death. This is why it is not something that is merely "tolerated" or "allowed", but it is also an act that is lawful in the eyes of God and that, when carried out in the proper form, is the fulfillment of a moral duty and is meritorious unto eternal life. The sexual act in marriage is chaste, because the virtue of chastity does not mean the exclusion of sexual pleasure, except when it is disordered or outside the normal context of marriage. This is the reason why *chastity can have two forms*: one that is proper to the unmarried—single or widowed persons—and another that corresponds to those who are married.

In marriage, not only sexual union itself is moral but also that which is conducive to it and which contributes to making it a physically and spiritually satisfying act of love. Either one of the spouses has the right to ask the other for the marital act or "conjugal debt", and the spouse to whom this request is made should not refuse, except for serious reasons. To deny a formal request would be sinful, and worse still if this refusal could be an occasion of sin for the other spouse. However, one spouse must not force this demand if it is clear that the other spouse has a serious reason for not agreeing. In all this, there is sensitivity in charity that should allow one to accept a refusal, even at the cost of a certain sacrifice.

On the other hand, there are unchaste acts, even within marriage, in which couples seek sexual pleasure *without performing the conjugal act, or when the act itself is performed in a way that intentionally or artificially deprives it of its procreative nature*. The latter occurs mainly when artificial contraceptives are used, which Catholic moral teaching has not approved as legitimate means [of regulating births].

In this area, and within the realm of what *is not permitted*, one should note that there are methods that are, strictly speaking, "contraceptive" because they impede in various ways the fertilization of the woman, whereas there are other methods that are really much worse than contraceptives because they do not prevent fertilization but instead provoke the loss of an already conceived fetus, albeit at the first stages of its development.

The latter are not contraceptives, strictly speaking, but

abortifacients [Spanish, *microabortivos*], which is to say that they produce tiny abortions. And because an assault on human life is a crime, *whatever the size of the human being who is killed*, the use of abortifacients is as serious as abortion itself, even if one's conscience is appeased by the fact that the woman does not realize what has happened or is uncertain about it. The so-called "*intrauterine devices*", or "*IUDs*" (in the shape of a ring, a spiral, or a copper T), are, according to reliable research, *abortifacient*.

The Church recognizes that spouses have the *right to regulate the number of their children for valid reasons*, about which they themselves must be the judges. But *they cannot do so by any means whatsoever*, because in this area, as in all human conduct, it is an immutable principle that "*the end does not justify the means.*"

An end can be as legitimate as you like, but that does not authorize you to attain it by any means whatsoever. A human act is *moral* when all three aspects are lawful: its *end*, *the means* by which that end is obtained, and *the circumstances* under which the act is accomplished. Giving alms out of vanity is an act that is morally vitiated in its end. The acquisition of an object that in itself is lawful to possess, but that is obtained by theft, is vitiated because of the means employed to get it. To hunt with firearms while endangering the lives of human beings is an act vitiated by that circumstance.

Catholic moral teaching allows, as a legitimate means of regulating births, the performance of the marital act on *those days when the woman is naturally infertile*. The problem lies, then, in determining the moment of ovulation, that is to say, the time when the mature egg detaches itself from the ovary and starts its journey toward the uterus. Since it is possible for the egg to be fertilized only during a few days, and since sperm, also, have a brief and determinate life span, it is possible to calculate when the infertile days will be, if one knows the time of ovulation.

There have been different methods of determining the moment of ovulation and, consequently, of the infertile days within a woman's menstrual period.

One, which presupposes the woman to have a very regular menstruation cycle, is based on counting the days, taking menstruation as the point of reference.

Another consists of making a daily record of the woman's temperature, since a slight rise in the basal temperature occurs at the moment of ovulation.

The third, and the most up-to-date and certain, is a matter of observing the cervical mucus, which is present in a woman's external organs on certain days of her menstrual period. There is a very exact connection between the consistency of this mucus and the moment of ovulation, so that this last can be deduced from an examination of the mucus, something that does not present difficulties for any woman.

This third method is useful not only in avoiding conception, but also in achieving it when children are desired, by performing the act at the most opportune time. Truly, it is wonderful how a woman's body is made to favor fertility by means of a secretion that helps the sperm to advance more effectively toward the egg that is capable of being fertilized.

There are times in which regulation of childbearing presents serious problems. In these cases the advice of a Catholic doctor who is well-informed about natural methods can be extremely helpful, especially in this third one, called the Billings method [3]—named after Doctors John and Evelyn Billings, a married couple who are both physicians, who

[3] See John D. Billings, *Ovulation Method: Natural Family Planning* (Collegeville, Minn.: Liturgical Press, 1984).

discovered it and have disseminated it throughout the world. The advice of a priest can also be very useful.

But it has to be emphasized again that the natural regulation of childbearing presupposes a well-formed *moral conscience* in both spouses and a *willingness to abstain* from sexual union during the woman's fertile days. The *discipline* acquired before marriage will be, as I have said, a very important element in making possible the application of these methods.

It is obvious that conjugal chastity demands keeping watch over one's affections, since human frailty can succumb to attractions that are incompatible with fidelity. It is particularly dangerous when, in moments of crisis or of serious disagreements, one of the spouses runs for comfort to a person of the opposite sex. Even in the absence of quarrels, it is always harmful to allow oneself to be carried away by feelings of excessive affection, which can lead to occasional or more ongoing infidelities. When one of the spouses has been unfaithful and this comes to be known by the other spouse, Christian charity and magnanimity counsel forgiving and forgetting, in order to save that essential unity founded on the sacrament, the bond of which ends only at death.

Let us say one last word about conjugal chastity, remembering the counsel of Saint Paul to practice, by mutual agreement, voluntary abstinence as a means of fostering dedication to prayer (see 1 Cor 7:2–5).

No hard-and-fast rules can be given here, only conduct that responds to the invitation of the Holy Spirit and does not impair the rights of the other spouse or put fidelity and purity at risk. This voluntary abstinence, which is not imposed but *freely assumed* at certain specific times, has a special spiritual value: it is like an affirmation, in deeds, of one's faith in eternal life and a sincere acceptance of the transience of our condition in this world (see Mt 22:29–30).

The ancient Toledo Rite inherited from the Church in Spain, which was still in use among us up to the time of the Second Vatican Council, publicly recommended to newly-weds, at the conclusion of the wedding ceremony, a greater moderation in the use of matrimony in the seasons when the liturgy of the Church especially invites the faithful to penance (Advent and Lent), and even abstinence on the vigils of major feast days. This recommendation was not a precept, but rather a *suggestion* left to the spiritual sensitivity of the Christian spouses. Today hardly anyone ventures to make this suggestion; nonetheless, it retains all of its value and meaning.

The positive outlook that the Church has on the orderly exercise of sexuality within marriage is expressed in a special prayer, which is included in the Roman ritual, whereby the *marriage bed is blessed*. It is an indication of how far the Church is from viewing with mistrust or misgivings what God has established as a manifestation of chaste love and as the origin of new life.

Many Christian couples place *in their bedroom an image* of our Lord Jesus Christ or of the Immaculate Virgin Mary, as though imploring them to bless their love. These images should be in every Catholic home and be a permanent invitation to a love that is chaste and faithful, joyful and self-sacrificing, here in this world and extending beyond it, between those who live, within the sacrament of matrimony, the mystery of love between God and his Church.

Marital chastity, far from being something that chills love, gives it the only true dignity that it has in God's eyes and leads to the discovery of a new depth in the practice of the charity-in-Christ that unites Christian spouses.

VIII. On Nullity of Marriage and on the
Dissolution of the Marital Bond

A Basic Definition of Terms

Now and then one hears the expression "So-and-so's marriage has been annulled by the Church." The expression is correct, but it is frequently *misunderstood*.

Let us recall, in the first place, that *a marriage celebrated by two baptized persons and consummated through normal sexual union cannot be dissolved by any human power, whether ecclesiastical or civil.* Or, to say the same thing differently, a validly contracted and consummated marriage is indissoluble until death, without any exception. This is a basic principle that is firmly upheld by the Church's Magisterium and that originates *not in any human law* enacted by Church authorities, *but rather in the Law of God,* over which the Church has no power whatsoever. Thus, in the highly unlikely event that some authority of the Church would assume for himself the right to dissolve a valid and consummated marriage, that act would be absolutely invalid and would constitute abuse of power having no effect in God's eyes. "What therefore God has joined together, let not man put asunder" (Mk 10:9). This is a saying of Christ, which the Church repeats every time the rite of marriage is celebrated.

Having said that, we must explain briefly what is involved in:

— A declaration of the nullity of a marriage by the tribunals of the Church;

— the dissolution of the marital bond between persons who have contracted marriage but have not consummated it;

— the so-called "Pauline privilege"; and

— the "privilege of the faith".

Nullity of a Christian Marriage

The annulment of a Christian marriage is the *declaration*, pronounced by the competent tribunals of the Church, that establishes that the marriage in question *never existed*, in other words, that it *was invalid from the beginning*, despite all *appearances* and notwithstanding the fact that the parties who considered themselves spouses may have done so in *good faith*. An ecclesiastical annulment *does not break* and cannot break a valid bond; the only thing that it does is to establish that the marriage bond that was thought to be valid *in reality never was valid, since it was vitiated* from the very moment when the matrimonial consent was given, which consent, for this reason, *could not effect* a true sacramental marriage. It is indispensable to understand this well. We must discard the notion some people have, who think that the Church can "undo" a valid marriage; this is a *grave error*. If the marriage was valid, was between two baptized people, and was consummated, the Church cannot "undo" it for *any reason whatsoever, even in tragic or very distressing situations.* The most that can be done in such cases is a separation of the spouses, but the marital bond remains permanently. *Neither one of them*, whether at fault or not, *can enter into a new marriage.*

This having been said, it is fair to ask what grounds can lead the Church to *declare that a marriage is null.* These grounds *had to exist at the time the marriage was contracted*, or seemed to be contracted. It is not enough for them to have arisen afterward; they must affect the constitution of the bond itself.

We cannot make a detailed examination of the reasons for nullity, since it is a very complex subject that presupposes a great deal of knowledge about canon law. We will limit ourselves, therefore, to giving a few examples that are usually the most common ones.

There are reasons for nullity directly affecting *the consent* given by the parties or by one of them. If a marriage is contracted in a gravely unjust manner, with the consent obtained by force, the marriage is invalid. It is invalid also if consent *was not given forever*, but was limited to a certain period only, or for as long as there would be harmony in the marriage. If the contracting parties excluded any *right to the procreation of children* [that is, had decided in advance not to have children], that marriage likewise is null. If one of the parties reserves for himself the *right* to have a lover, that consent is invalid. It is invalid also, if there is an *error as to the identity* of one of the spouses, admittedly an unlikely event.

Other reasons for annulment arise from the fact that there was an *impediment to marriage* for which a dispensation was not obtained or could not be obtained. If one of the spouses is *impotent*, that is, incapable of performing a normal and complete sexual act with the other spouse, and if that incapacity is permanent, the marriage is null and void. But *we must not confuse impotence with sterility*. The latter means that, although a normal sexual act can be performed, this act is not generative (or fruitful) due to organic or physiological defects. Impotence cannot be dispensed.

Another impediment to a valid marriage is the existence of *close kinship* between the spouses (cousins, uncle and niece, father-in-law and daughter-in-law), although this impediment can be dispensed. *Disparity of cult*, meaning that one of the contracting parties is baptized and the other is not, or *mixed religion*, that is to say, the fact that one of the contracting parties is Catholic and the other belongs to another non-Catholic Christian confession, are impediments to marriage. However, disparity of cult is a reason for nullity only in a marriage that was contracted without the required dispensation. There is a very serious canonical impediment to a marriage, called the impediment "of crime", which declares that a married person who has killed his or her spouse cannot enter into a valid marriage with the accomplice to the crime.

There are other similar cases in keeping with this impediment. There is also an impediment to marriage between *an abductor and the woman he has abducted* for as long a time as the latter is in the possession of the former. The Church has established a *minimum age* requirement for a marriage to be valid. As you can see, the impediments established by the Church are intended to *safeguard the sanctity of marriage.*

Finally, there can be grounds for nullity in the *absence of the minimal formalities* established by the Church for matrimonial consent. In all but very exceptional cases, said consent must be expressed before the parish priest or another authorized priest [or deacon] and before two witnesses. One can understand the Church's vigilance, so as to ensure that consent is given publicly and can be proven if necessary.

When one petitions the tribunals of the Church for a declaration of nullity of a marriage, it is not enough to state that said marriage is null and void; it is necessary to *prove it* by means of documents, witnesses, expert testimony, and so on. Should these proofs be false, the nullity declared would have, *in conscience, no worth whatsoever.*

Given that the Church is very concerned that the grounds for nullity be aired openly and with all possible diligence, the judgment given in the first instance does not suffice; this judgment *must be reviewed by a second tribunal.* If both judgments declare the nullity of the marriage, the presumptive spouses are then free to enter into a new marriage. If one of the judgments declares the nullity and the other does not, an appeal to a third tribunal can be commenced.

Every country has, generally speaking, tribunals of the first and of the second instance; any further appeal (that is, the third instance) is normally within the competence of the Roman tribunals, the Holy Roman Rota. In every instance there is an ecclesiastical official whose task it is to *defend the validity of the marriage* for which a declaration of nullity is sought; this is one more guarantee to preserve the validity and indissolubility of marriage. Of course, both parties have the right to a defense of their case by legal counsel expert in the laws of the Church and in the jurisprudence of the ecclesiastical tribunals. This legal counsel can be either a priest or a layman.

Dissolution of the Marriage Bond

We said at the beginning of this chapter that if a marriage was contracted by two baptized persons and was subsequently consummated by means of a normal sexual act, such a bond cannot be dissolved by any human power. However, *if either of these two elements is missing*, the baptism of both parties or the consummation, the marriage thus contracted is not entirely indissoluble, but rather, *in certain cases, can be dissolved*. Let us look at the three cases in which Catholic doctrine allows and pronounces the dissolution of the marriage bond.

The first case is that of a marriage which is said to be *"ratified and non-consummated"*. It is assumed that the contracting parties have validly expressed their consent and that they are baptized. However, they have not engaged in sexual union, not because of impotence (for that would be grounds for nullity), but for other reasons. It is not a common occurrence, but it can happen, and it does happen. In this case both parties, or one of them, can *have recourse to the Pope, requesting that he "dispense" or dissolve this marriage*. Here *it is not a matter of nullity*, since the marriage is valid, but rather of a *dispensation from the bond*, granted by the Pope.

For the Pope to be able to grant this dissolution of the marital bond, it is necessary that the petition be made to the Ordinary of the place where the parties reside.

On the authority of the Ordinary, a legal proceeding is initiated for the purpose of ascertaining that the marriage has not, in fact, been consummated. The acts of this proceeding, together with the opinion of the Ordinary, are then sent to Rome, indicating the *serious reasons* that motivate the petition, and the Holy Father, once he has examined the case, either grants the dispensation or does not.

There is another situation in which a ratified and non-consummated marriage can be dissolved, even without papal dispensation, and this occurs when one of the parties makes a solemn profession in a religious order.

The second case is that of the "*Pauline privilege*", so-called because it is derived from a passage by Saint Paul (1 Cor 7:12–15). Here it is assumed that two persons married when both were non-Christians and therefore not baptized. If one of the spouses is then baptized and *the other remains non-baptized and departs*, the baptized spouse has the right to marry another person, and when this new marriage is contracted, the first one is dissolved. It is understood that the non-baptized spouse "departs" when he in fact does not consent to live with the spouse who has received baptism, or when he does not accept a peaceful coexistence that does not offend God.

In any case, it is necessary that the non-baptized spouse be interpellated, that is, formally questioned as to whether he wants to receive baptism or, at least, is willing to live together with the other spouse peacefully, without offense to God. This "interpellation" is usually done through the local

Ordinary; if that is not possible, it can be done privately, but in such a way that it is possible to prove the ill will on the part of the non-baptized spouse.

The third case, called *"privilege of faith"*, occurs when the marriage has been contracted validly between two persons, *one of whom is baptized and the other is not.* In such a case, and for serious reasons, the baptized person can petition the Pope to *dissolve* this marriage.

As you can see, the dissolution of a "ratified and non-consummated" marriage is based on the failure to consummate it; in the case of the Pauline privilege and the privilege of the faith, the possibility of dissolving the marriage springs from the absence of baptism in one of the parties. In the dissolution of a ratified and non-consummated marriage and in the dissolution of a marriage because of the privilege of the faith, the Holy Father is the one who makes the decision. In the case of the Pauline privilege, it is not necessary for the matter to go to Rome.

When one encounters a case such as those described above, the correct and prudent thing to do is to have recourse to an expert in canon law, and not to consider things to be resolved according to superficial opinions or sentimental reasons. In every diocese there are competent persons who can be consulted in these matters.

IX. Divorce

The word *divorce* is used to designate several very different things. In Chilean civil law, a divorce, which can be temporary or permanent, consists of an interruption of the spouses' life together, in compliance with a court decision. But this kind of "divorce" does not dissolve the marital bond; the "divorced" parties continue to be man and wife and cannot remarry. This situation is analogous to the one provided for by canon law, in which it is referred to as "separation of the spouses".

Incorrectly, but usually called "divorce", too, is a "nullity of civil marriage" pronounced by a civil court, generally on false grounds adduced by witnesses who are also false. This is the status of civil law in Chile.

But there are countries, very many of them, in which civil law permits spouses to divorce civilly, terminating the bond and enabling them to remarry. The grounds for these divorces range from adultery and ill treatment to incompatibility and even mutual agreement.

The Church's Position

The Catholic Church allows couples, for serious reasons, to *stop living together.* The Church does not want this, and she recommends doing everything possible to restore unity and life in common, exhorting spouses to practice forgiveness, patience, and charity. If it happens, unfortunately, that cohabitation is discontinued—assuming that the marriage is valid and has not been declared null by the Church—the separated spouses *continue to be husband and wife, continue to be united by the marital bond, and are still obliged, both of them, to remain faithful.*

If they resort to a civil "annulment", or if they divorce in such a way as to dissolve the bond (in countries where this has been established by law), *that "annulment" or "divorce" is without effect with regard to the conscience of the spouses* (even if they believe the contrary), or before the Church or before God; *they continue to be married to each other,* for no human authority can separate what God has united.

If the "divorcé(e)" has sexual relations with a third party, he or she *commits adultery* with the third party. If, despite the sacramental bond that persists, someone who has divorced civilly contracts civil marriage with a third person, that civil marriage has no validity whatsoever in the eyes of the Catholic faith and of the Church; it only serves to produce some civil effects, but at the cost of establishing a bond before human law, which basically *consolidates a permanent state of adultery*.

The position of the Catholic Church has been *very firm in this respect*, and the popes have vigorously defended the indissolubility of marriage, even at the cost of terrible calamities, as in the case of King Henry VIII of England or in the case of the emperor Napoleon I. Unfortunately, other Christian communities, such as the Orthodox churches and the Protestant denominations, have not maintained the same firmness. Whatever may be the reasons for or consequences of the Church's uncompromising stance, the *Church cannot make concessions in this matter*, for she is dealing with a law of God, over which she has no control.

The Church *cannot consider legitimate* a union that disregards the indissolubility of marriage and *cannot* in any way *compare it* to a lawful sacramental marriage; she *cannot even regard it as having any legitimacy* or act as if such unions were acceptable.

And when we say "the Church", we are not referring only to the ecclesiastical authorities, but also to the faithful who adhere, as is their obligation, to the Catholic doctrine on marriage.

If it happened that someone did not adhere to it, we would be in the presence of a grave defect in the communion of faith.

Some people, even some who call themselves Catholic,

do not understand this position of the Church and consider it "narrow-minded", or "rigid", or "intolerant", or even "cruel". These opinions generally spring from the compassion evoked by the very painful situations of some husbands and wives who, sometimes through no fault of their own, have seen their homes destroyed.

This feeling of compassion is quite legitimate, but *it cannot lead us to change God's law and to stop calling what is sinful a sin.*

These persons forget that, just as God has every right to dispose of our life when, where, and as he pleases, he also has the right to demand of us heroic acts, which may be as painful as the loss of life itself. If this were not the case, there would have been no martyrs in the Church. When God demands heroic fidelity from a Christian, he will also grant to him the grace to accept his will and to resist temptation: "God is faithful, and he will not let you be tempted beyond your strength, but with the temptation will also provide the way of escape [or the strength], that you may be able to endure it" (1 Cor 10:13).

The words of Saint Paul have a very fitting application here: "None of us lives to himself, and none of us dies to himself. If we live, we live to the Lord, and if we die, we die to the Lord; so then, whether we live or whether we die, we are the Lord's" (Rom 14:7-8).

The doctrine of the Church on the indissolubility and fidelity of marriage should be *seriously considered* by those who wish to contract this sacred bond, in keeping with what has been said in the third and fourth chapters. The tragic consequences of a failed marriage should help us reflect profoundly and in the presence of God, so as not to take any foolhardy risks. And when a split does occur, then it will be necessary more than ever to have recourse to the fountains of grace, prayer, penance, and the sacraments, so as to live as a Christian in a painful solitude, which nonetheless can be a *great testimony to faith and love* for God and for his holy law.

The Situation of Divorced Persons Who Have Remarried

The introduction of civil divorce laws, resulting in the [civil] dissolution of the marital bond, or of fraudulent "annulments", which come to the same thing, has weakened in many Christians the sense of the indissolubility of marriage. Society today, for various reasons, no longer finds these situations all that problematic. But a Catholic cannot help wondering just what is the situation of a person who, having joined with another through the sacrament of matrimony, has had a civil divorce or annulment, and then remarried, that is, contracted a civil bond with a third person.

Let us repeat briefly the principles of Catholic doctrine in this regard:

— Civil annulment or divorce *has no effect whatsoever on the sacred bond of matrimony; it neither dissolves nor annuls it.*
— *Only the authority of the Church is competent to declare the nullity of a marriage between two believers*, and to this same authority are reserved the exceptional cases of dissolving the marital bond that is ratified but not consummated or by the privilege of the faith.
— For a person married in the Church and divorced to live together with a third person *is, morally speaking, a sin of adultery*, whether or not there is a civil bond of marriage.

The first conclusion to be drawn from the preceding is that it is an aberration for persons who are about to embark on a life of adultery to ask the Church to "*bless*" this new *unlawful and sinful* union. It is actually a sacrilege to try to "bless" what is a sin in the eyes of God.

No "human" consideration can authorize such a transaction, and if it were to take place, it would be not only *disloyalty to the law of God* but also an act that would give rise to a *very serious confusion* among the faithful: as though there were two levels of lawful union between a man and a woman: sacramental marriage and civil marriage, which renders "legitimate" a merely human living arrangement between two baptized persons.

Let us recall that between Christians there is no valid marriage that is not, at the same time, the sacrament of Jesus Christ. The Permanent Committee of the Chilean Bishops Conference was quite right in having a declaration published that determines that such "blessings" are *prohibited* and that to carry them out is a grave offense against ecclesiastical discipline.

Those who have taken the step of entering into an unlawful union must realize that their action is not acceptable and that they must respect the law of God, at least by *not pretending that their situation has been accepted as lawful*. An attitude of humility could be the start along the path of conversion, of penance, and of making decisions consistent with the faith.

Since these persons are in a situation that, objectively, is a *state of sin*, it will not be possible for them, as long as they live as husband and wife, to be absolved from their sins or to receive Holy Communion. If they were to receive absolution under these conditions, *that absolution would be invalid*, because the forgiveness of sins presupposes repentance or contrition, which is a hatred and "detestation of sin committed, with a determination of not sinning in the future" (Council of Trent), and in the case of these persons this repentance does not exist. It follows that denying absolution to them is *not something that depends on the judgment of the priest*, but rather on the very nature of the sacrament of penance; the forgiveness of sins *is not an arbitrary act of the confessor, but rather results conjointly from the dispositions of the penitent and the priestly absolution.*

If the proper dispositions of the penitent, especially contrition and the resolution of amendment, are not present, *nothing can substitute for them.* If there is genuine repentance and a firm resolution of amendment, the confessor must give the absolution; if they are lacking, absolution cannot be given, and if given anyway, it is invalid.

Since we are dealing with something that does not depend upon the authority of the Church, *it is not possible to allow exceptions for special cases* or to grant "permission" to receive Holy Communion, "even in a single instance". We repeat: this is not a question of the more or less "open-minded" judgment of the priest, but rather a doctrinal matter.

If someone claims that he has received "permission" in this regard, he has either misunderstood the priest, or else the priest who gave the "permission" was wrong and exceeded his competence or departed from the doctrine of the Church, thereby committing an abuse.

In Chile, the bishops have judged that fraudulent annulments of civil marriage are a calamity that has serious consequences for society, and therefore they have thus punished it with sentence of *excommunication.*[4] This penalty was established for the first time by means of an unanimous agreement by the bishops in 1941. Later it was confirmed and broadened in the First Plenary Council of Chile, promulgated in 1955.

Subject to this penalty are both those who fraudulently annul their civil marriages, having been married in the Church, and also those who cooperate in the fraud. If, after

---

[4] That was the situation in 1981, the year in which then-Bishop Medina wrote this text.— ED.

having obtained this fraudulent annulment, they contract a civil marriage to a third person, they incur a *second excommunication*, which applies also to the witnesses to the act.

If these penalties were to be abolished, and the Church could do so,[5] that would in no way change the sinful state of these persons, nor would they be permitted to go to Communion, since *the eventual suppression of a canonical penalty does not mean that the sin, which is against the law of God, has ceased to be a sin.*

Yet excommunication is not a punishment that has to last a lifetime. If the one who is affected by this sentence *truly repents and stops sinning*, absolution can be obtained, both from the excommunication and also from the sin. Because of the delicate nature of these absolutions, they are reserved to bishops, to their vicars, and to some priests who have special faculties.

The reconciliation of these persons with God and with the Church, if it is the case that they have contracted a new civil marriage, can take place *when they definitively cease living together and having conjugal relations.* This occurs through the death of one of them or by means of an actual separation—whether by living apart from each other or, if that is impossible (because they have children, for example), then by living under the same roof, but without continuing to have marital relations, that is, by practicing continence.

It still remains for us to examine the situation of such persons *as they relate to other Christians.* This is an extremely delicate and complex problem. Two important principles are

---

[5] As it happened, a few years after this work was published, in March 1984, a total derogation [revocation] of the First Plenary Council of Chile was promulgated, as granted by Pope John Paul II, at the request of the Bishops Conference of Chile. This revocation includes the suppression of the excommunications mentioned above. This change is in keeping with the reduction of the excommunications in the Code of Canon Law of 1983.— ED.

at stake. The *first is the principle of charity toward such persons*, a charity that can oblige us to deal with them at different levels, even at the level of friendship. The *second is the principle of fidelity to the truth*, a fidelity that *prevents us from accepting these couples as if they were joined in a true marriage*, and as if their situation were acceptable and not sinful.

We should recognize how difficult it is to harmonize these two principles in practice. If the former is taken to the extreme, one runs the risk of eliminating the second, and vice versa. And there is no doubt as to the seriousness of the problem, that attitudes in society, little by little, are becoming so broad and so "tolerant" that, *in practice, these unlawful unions have come to be considered as legitimate, acceptable, and moral.*

One must distinguish also between public acts, in which it is not possible to enforce the principles of the Church, and everyday family life, in which, even though it cause great sorrow, *the comparison between matrimony and unlawful unions cannot be accepted.*

In the latter sphere we ought not to forget *the formation of the children's conscience*; if they see that divorced and remarried couples are accepted in the same way as persons living in a true marriage, it will be very difficult to make them understand later on, in a moment of crisis in their own marriage, that seeking a civil annulment and subsequent remarriage is not acceptable conduct for a Catholic.

All that has been said is enough to make clear how sad the situation of these persons is, a situation that, to the extent that they keep the faith, assumes tragic and extremely painful proportions. One should meditate on this in moments when a crisis threatens a marriage, and make *then and there* every effort to save the union, and not allow oneself to be lured into the real trap, which would be a fraudulent civil annulment and a subsequent civil union with a person other than one's lawful spouse. There is no sacrifice that would be too great when safeguarding the unity of the home.

Pastoral Approach to These Persons

However severe the doctrine of the Church may be, and even though she cannot compromise on the principles that proceed from the law of God, that does not mean that persons in the situation described above must be rejected absolutely. Let us enumerate some doctrinal elements that will then serve as a basis for some pastoral guidelines.

— These individuals, despite their sin and even their status as excommunicated persons,[6] *have not stopped being Christians*, for baptism cannot be obliterated, and it is quite possible that they have kept the faith.

— "The Church *clasps . . . sinners to her bosom*" (LG, no. 8), and has in their regard the *duty* to pray for their conversion and to help them (LG, no. 11).

— These persons are *not prohibited from attending* the preaching of the Word of God or the celebration of the Holy Mass, even though they cannot receive the sacraments.

— Despite their state of sin, *they still have many Christian duties*—in the first place, the duty of seeking their own conversion, but also that of praying, of practicing charity, and of educating their children in a Christian and Catholic way, even when these children were born of an unlawful union.

— It is a question, then, of "*sick members*" of the Church, who are incapacitated and thus unable to take on all of their religious responsibilities or to exercise all the rights pertaining to normal membership in the Church.

---

[6] Although this excommunication is no longer in force, the principles stated by Cardinal Medina preserve their general validity.— Ed.

— Consequently, the Church must *provide them with pastoral care* to help them fulfill their obligations; *this support*, however, *does not signify and should not be interpreted as the acceptance or legitimization* of their situation. A misunderstanding of this sort would be harmful to the faith of the community, toward which there is also a duty of charity. Here prudence plays an important role.

— These persons *cannot take on pastoral or official apostolic responsibilities*, such as those of catechists, lectors at Holy Mass, extraordinary ministers of the Eucharist, leaders of pastoral movements, and religion teachers, because these duties would be, in some way, legitimizing their situation in the sight of the rest of the faithful.

These elementary points either are Church teaching or else are derived from it; all that being understood, a field (albeit *limited*) remains open for the pastoral care of these persons. The first step in this care must be to bring them to *acknowledge the irregularity of their situation before God and the Church* and to accept the consequences of it, without trying to force the Church or her clergy to tell them that what is wrong according to the law of God is all right in their case.

This acknowledgment is a major step toward conversion: the *conviction that one has sinned* begins to form, and keeping this in mind is important along the road of repentance. This acknowledgment ought to lead logically to the decision *not to appear together in Church*, which would come to be an initial way, although external and not entirely sufficient, of showing *repentance*. This first step could be the fruit of apostolic work by laymen and also of the help of priests who, very patiently but firmly, manage to disenchant them of their desire to justify themselves.

Once this first step has been taken, others could follow. One would have to make sure that these persons reestablish *contact with the Word of God* through the reading of Sacred Scripture. This contact would necessarily clear the way to the humble practice of *prayer*, in the spirit of the publican of whom the Gospel speaks (Lk 18:9–14).

Together with this could come a strengthening of the sense of *repentance*, perhaps in the form of the voluntary renunciation of things that are in themselves legitimate, as an expression of the desire to make reparation for sins committed and to fortify the will.

The priest, *while avoiding any ambivalent attitude* that could lend itself to being interpreted as a sacramental absolution, could attend to these persons, helping them to turn back to God, through a form of "spiritual direction". The *practice of charity*, in all its forms, would have a special importance for these persons, since "love covers a multitude of sins" (1 Pet 4:8).

Either one or both of the persons who find themselves in the situation described can be "put back on the right track" in this way. If it is only one of them, the road will be more difficult, but should not therefore be neglected. If both take part, given the initial acknowledgment that we have described, there would be no objection to the priest receiving them together, but privately.

It does not seem advisable to organize special groups of persons in this situation. That has many disadvantages: it creates the appearance of a sort of *official "status"*, it runs the risk of developing *pressure groups*, it gives the impression that the members form a "subculture", and it fosters public discussion of a wide variety of matters and situations that are very delicate and intimate. Perhaps, though, one could occasionally, with discretion, hold meetings on the subject that will not lend themselves to misunderstandings.

Once a certain level of spiritual life has been reached,

these persons are basically in a position, although imperfect and by no means ideal, to take on apostolic responsibility in the family catechesis of their children. They ought to assume it with confidence in the mercy of God and with the certainty that he can and wants to make use of them for the work of the first proclamation of the faith. A time will come when they will have to explain their situation to their children. That will be a very distressing and delicate moment.

They will have to face up to it with the help of prayer and with great humility, and if they do so, no doubt it will be a very powerful and valid testimony to their faith, which will make a profound impression on their children and make them respect their parents, who are capable of recognizing their errors for the love of God. *The truth is more important than excuses and pretexts.*

It is possible that this moment would be excessively difficult, and in that case one could ask a brother in faith to explain to the children, with sensitivity, the situation of their parents.

A process of maturing in faith, shared by both, and prepared with all the spiritual resources detailed above, should culminate in an *act* which is *heroic, but possible*: the mutual decision to *discontinue all marital relations and cohabitation.*

God only knows how difficult it is to take this step, but he will grant the necessary grace to those who have prepared themselves for it by prayer and penance. When this decision has been taken, a decision that is noble and beautiful in the eyes of God, *the time will have come to approach the sacrament of penance,* so as humbly to ask forgiveness for sins, and to receive it through the absolution given by the priest.

Thus *the door will be open for them to be able to receive Holy Communion.* But it should not be received in public, because of the scandal that could be given to persons who are unaware of what has taken place in secret in the consciences of the couple.

If somehow it came to be known that they have gone to Communion, it would be their duty to *declare, with delicacy and humility, that their marital cohabitation has ended*, and that it is due to this, and not to any sort of "tolerance" or "permission", that they have been able to return to the sacraments.

In that case, and with the necessary prudence, these persons could take a *more active part in the apostolic and pastoral life of the Church*, provided that they make clear what their new situation is.

It is evident that, in this delicate problem of pastoral care for persons in the situation described, one must proceed according to the directives of the bishops who, with pastoral prudence, determine the advisable course of action in their dioceses, within the guidelines that have been set forth. In this field, as in many others, it is absolutely essential to have uniform criteria and policies, and *not to act on feelings or allow oneself to be guided by examples that are not in keeping with Catholic doctrine.*

All of the preceding confirms that there are no easy solutions for serious problems. Yet it is reassuring to see that these solutions *are actually possible*, with the grace of God.

Conclusion

The history of the Church records the names of many Christians who attained sanctity in the state of holy matrimony. Let us recall the Blessed Virgin Mary and Saint Joseph; Saint Monica, the pious mother of Saint Augustine, and Blessed Joan of Aza, mother of Saint Dominic; the kings Saint Ferdinand I of Castile and Saint Louis IX of France; Saint Elizabeth of Portugal and Saint Elizabeth of Hungary, who were aunt and niece; the emperors of Germany Saint Henry II and his wife, Saint Cunegund; Saint Isidore, a humble laborer, and his wife, Saint María de la Cabeza; Saint Anna Maria Taigi, who counseled families.

Among the martyrs there were many married persons, such as Saint Leonides, father of the great theologian Origen, and Saint Felicity, who died for the faith shortly after giving birth to a son.

Some saints started the road to Christian perfection while married and then, when they were widowed, consecrated their lives in one or another religious order; for example, Saint Francis Borgia, Saint Jane Frances Frémyot de Chantal, Saint Joan de Lestonnac, and Saint Frances of Rome. They are legion, the faithful who have not been canonized by the Church but the memory of whose heroic testimony and Christian virtues has nevertheless been preserved as, for example, the parents of Saint Thérèse of Lisieux.

Léon Bloy said that "there is only one affliction in life: that of not being saints". Indeed, holiness is not at odds with joy; on the contrary, sanctity is the source of the most profound happiness.

Of course a state of life such as marriage, elevated by Jesus Christ to the dignity of a sacrament, has to be a nursery of saints! How could it be otherwise? Are not the sacraments channels and instruments of the grace that heals the wounds of sins and leads us to intimacy with God, to sanctity?

The supernatural dignity of Christian marriage is often forgotten, and perhaps that is the reason why many married people are not even aware that this state of life is a path to Christian perfection.

What a mistake it is to think that sanctity is attainable only by those who consecrate their lives in the priesthood or in religious life and to consider marriage as a sort of consecration to mediocrity! Holiness is one, as the Second Vatican Council teaches, but there are many roads leading to it, and charity and the Cross of Christ accompany them all.

It would be consoling if the perusal of the preceding, and even more so, of the writings of the Pastors of the Church that follow immediately after this—the reading of which we fervently recommend—would awaken in many engaged and married Christian couples an awareness of their vocation to holiness! Then many evils in this world would be remedied, and the Church could rejoice in seeing an abundant flowering of priestly and religious vocations, the natural fruit of Christian homes.

Some will say that in what has been written there is too much "idealism". Yes, why deny it? But then are not we priests witnesses to the fidelity of countless Christian spouses to the Lord? Have we not touched, so to speak, the heroic fortitude of so many fathers and mothers, husbands and wives?

If anyone is frightened by the Christian ideal, let him not forget the forceful, confident words of Saint Paul the Apostle: "I can do all things in him who strengthens me" (Phil 4:13).

CHAPTER TWO

The Catholic Doctrine on Marriage

I. Institution

The Divine and Human Transcendence of Marriage

The marriage covenant is founded on the preexisting, permanent structures that establish the difference between man and woman. It is also desired by the spouses as an institution, even though it is subject, in its concrete form, to various historical and cultural changes, as well as to particular personal characteristics. Thus the marital covenant is an institution desired by God himself, the Creator, with a view both to the help that the spouses must give to one another in love and fidelity, and also to the formation that must be given, within the familial community, to the children born of this union.

Marriage in Christ

The New Testament clearly shows that Jesus confirmed this institution, which had existed "from the beginning", and that he cured it of its subsequent defects (Mk 10:2–9; 10–12). Thus he restored it to its complete dignity, undiminished, and its initial requirements. Jesus sanctified this state of life

A study prepared by Cardinal Medina for the International Theological Commission in 1978— ED.

(GS, no. 48, 2) embedding it in the mystery of love that unites him, as Redeemer, with his Church. It is for this reason that the pastoral guidance and the regulation of Christian marriage have been entrusted to the Church (see 1 Cor 7:10–16).

The Apostles

The Epistles of the New Testament demand that all have respect for marriage (Heb 13:4), and, in response to certain attacks, they present it as a good work of God the Creator (1 Tim 4:1–5). They declare the value of marriage between faithful Christians, thanks to its insertion into the mystery of the covenant and the love that unite Christ with the Church (Eph 5:22–33; see GS, no. 48, 2). Consequently, they expect that marriage be realized "in the Lord" (1 Cor 7:39), and that the life of the spouses be led according to their dignity as a "new creation" (2 Cor 5:17) in Christ (Eph 5:21–33). They put the faithful on guard against pagan customs in this matter (1 Cor 6:12–20; 6:9–10). The apostolic churches are based upon a "law which has emanated from the faith" and want to ensure its permanence; in this sense, they formulate moral directives (Col 3:18ff.; Tit 2:3–5; 1 Pet 3:1–7) and issue judicial provisions aimed at fostering marital life "according to the faith" in various human situations and circumstances.

The First Centuries

During the first centuries of the history of the Church, Christians performed their wedding ceremonies "as other men do" (*Letter to Diognetus* 5, 6) with the father of the family presiding, accompanied only by customary gestures and rites such as, for example, that of joining the hands of the future spouses. They did not lose sight, however, of "the exceptional and truly paradoxical laws of their spiritual republic" (ibid., 5, 4). They eliminated from their domestic liturgy every trace of pagan religion. They attached particular importance to the procreation and education of children (ibid., 5, 6) and accepted the oversight exercised by the bishops over marriage (Ignatius of Antioch, *Letter to Polycarp* 5, 2). They manifested, through their marriage, a special subjection to God and a relationship with their faith (Clement of Alexandria, *Stromata* 4, 20). Occasionally, they even rejoiced in the celebration of the Eucharistic Sacrifice and of a special blessing on the occasion of their marriage (Tertullian, *Letter to His Wife* 2, 9).

The Eastern Traditions

In the churches of the East, from a very early age, pastors took an active part in the celebration of weddings, whether in place of the heads of the families or jointly with them. This change was not the result of a usurpation; on the contrary, it came about at the request of the families and with the approval of the civil authorities. Because of this evolution, the ceremonies that originally were carried out in the bosom of the family were progressively included in the liturgical rites themselves; accordingly, the view developed that the ministers of the rite of the matrimonial "mysterion" were not only the spouses, but also the pastor of the Church.

The Western Traditions

In the churches of the West, the Christian view of marriage encountered the Roman law. From this arose the question:

"What is the constitutive element of marriage from the juridical point of view?" This question was resolved in such a way that the consent of the spouses was considered the one constitutive element. That is why, up to the time of the Council of Trent, clandestine marriages were considered valid. Nevertheless, the Church had asked, for a long time, that a place be reserved for certain liturgical rites, for the blessing of the priest, and for his presence as the witness of the Church. Through the decree *"Tametsi"*, the presence of the parish priest and of other witnesses came to be the ordinary canonical form necessary for the validity of a marriage.

The New Churches

It is desirable that, under the supervision of the ecclesiastical authorities, new liturgical and juridical norms for Christian marriage be established among peoples that have recently been evangelized. The Second Vatican Council itself and the new rite for the celebration of matrimony call for them. In this way, the reality of Christian marriage will be harmonized with the authentic values manifested in the traditions of these peoples.

This diversity of norms due to the plurality of cultures is compatible with the essential unity [of the sacrament], since it does not exceed the limits of a legitimate pluralism.

The Christian and ecclesial character of the union and of the mutual self-giving of spouses can indeed be expressed in different ways, under the guidance of the baptism they have received and through the presence of witnesses, among whom the "competent priest" plays a very important part.

It may perhaps be deemed suitable to make various canonical adaptations of these different elements.

Canonical Adaptations

Any reform in canon law must take into account the overall vision of matrimony and its dimensions, both personal and social. The Church must be aware that juridical provisions are intended to help and promote conditions that are ever more attentive to the human values of marriage. It must not be supposed, however, that such adaptations can alter the reality of marriage in its totality.

The Institution Is Directed to the Person

"Insofar as man by his very nature stands completely in need of life in society, he is and he ought to be the beginning, the subject, and the object of every social organization" (GS, no. 25). As an "intimate partnership of married life and love" (GS, no. 48), marriage constitutes a place and a means suitable for promoting the good of persons along the path of their vocation. Consequently, marriage must never be considered a way of sacrificing persons to a common good that is extrinsic to them. Furthermore, the common good is "the sum total of social conditions which allow people, either as groups or as individuals, to reach their fulfillment more fully and more easily" (GS, no. 26).

A Structure, Not a Superstructure

Although marriage is subject to economic realities, both at the outset and throughout its duration, marriage is not a superstructure of the private property that consists of goods and resources. It is true that the concrete forms of marital and familial life can depend upon economic conditions. But the definitive union of a man and a woman in the marital covenant corresponds above all to human nature and to the requirements inscribed within it by the Creator. This is the profound reason why marriage, far from hindering maturity, greatly promotes the personal development of the spouses.

II. Sacramentality

A Real Symbol and a Sacramental Sign

Jesus Christ, in a prophetic way, brought about a rediscovery of the reality of marriage as God had intended it from the beginning of the human race (cf. Gen 1:27 = Mk 10:6 par.; Mt 19:4; cf. Gen 2:24 = Mk 10:7–8 par.; Mt 19:5). He restored it through his death and resurrection. Christian marriage, too, is lived "in the Lord" (1 Cor 7:39); its form is determined by the elements of the work of salvation.

Ever since the Old Testament, marital union has been a sign of the covenant between God and the people of Israel (see Hos 2; Jer 3:6–13; Ezek 16, 23; Is 54). In the New Testament, marriage assumes an even loftier dignity, since it is the representation of the mystery that unites Jesus Christ with the Church (see Eph 5:21–33). This analogy is illuminated in greater depth by means of theological interpretation: the unsurpassable love and the gift of God, even to the shedding of his blood, together with the faithful and irrevocable adherence of the Church, his Spouse, become the model and example for Christian marriage. This likeness is a relation of authentic participation in the covenant of love between Christ and the Church. For its part, inasmuch as it is a real symbol and a sacramental sign, Christian marriage represents in concrete terms the Church of Jesus Christ in the world and, above all with respect to the family, is rightly called "the domestic Church" (LG, no. 11).

A Sacrament in the Strict Sense

In the way that has been explained, Christian marriage is configured with the mystery of the union between Jesus Christ and the Church. The fact that Christian matrimony is thus taken up into the economy of salvation already justifies its designation as a "sacrament" in a wider sense. But even more than that, it is a concrete crystallization and a real actualization of this fundamental sacrament [or "mystery"]. Accordingly, Christian marriage is in itself, truly and properly, a sign of salvation that confers the grace of Jesus Christ, and that is why the Catholic Church numbers it among the seven sacraments (DS 1327, 1801).

There is a specific connection, that is to say, an essential and reciprocal relationship, between the indissolubility of marriage and its sacramentality. Its indissolubility allows us to perceive more easily the sacramentality of Christian marriage and, vice versa, from the theological point of view, its sacramentality constitutes the ultimate ground, though not the only one, for the indissolubility of marriage.

Baptism, Existing Faith, Intention, Sacramental Marriage

Like the other sacraments, matrimony also communicates grace. The ultimate source of this grace is the effect of the work accomplished by Jesus Christ and not merely the faith of the subjects of the sacrament. This does not mean, however, that in the sacrament of matrimony grace is conferred upon those whose faith is marginal or nonexistent. Hence it follows, according to classic principles, that faith is a prerequisite, also termed a "dispositive cause", of the fruitful reception of the sacrament. Yet, on the other hand, the validity of the sacrament does not depend upon whether or not it is fruitful.

The fact that there are "baptized non-believers" today poses a new theological problem and a serious pastoral dilemma, especially if the absence and even the rejection of faith seem to be evident. The required intention—the intention of accomplishing what Christ and the Church accomplish—is the minimum requirement in order for there to be a genuine human act of commitment at the level of the sacramental reality. Of course, one should not confuse the question about the intention with the problem concerning the faith of the contracting parties. Neither can they be separated completely, however. Ultimately, the genuine intention springs from and is nourished by a living faith. Where one cannot perceive any vestige of faith as such (in the sense of "belief", that is, a willingness to believe), or any desire for grace and salvation, this poses the problem of knowing, at the factual level, whether the general and truly sacramental intention, which we have been discussing, is present or not, and whether the marriage has been validly contracted or not. The personal faith of the contracting parties, as we have demonstrated, does not make the marriage a sacramental one, but the absence of personal faith jeopardizes the validity of the sacrament.

This fact raises further questions, to which adequate answers have not as yet been found; this fact also imposes new pastoral responsibilities in dealing with Christian marriage. "Above all, it is imperative that pastors make an effort to develop and nourish the faith of the engaged couple, because the sacrament of matrimony presupposes and requires faith" (*Ordo celebrandi matrimonium*, Praenotanda, no. 7).

A Dynamic Articulation

In the Church, baptism is the social foundation and the sacrament of faith, by virtue of which human beings who believe become members of the Body of Christ. From this point of view, also, the existence of "baptized non-believers" implies problems of great importance. Pastoral and practical necessities will not find a real solution in changes that eliminate the central core of [Catholic] doctrine concerning the sacraments [in general] and marriage [in particular], but rather in a radical renewal of baptismal spirituality. It is necessary to restore an integral vision that sees baptism within the essential unity and the dynamic articulation of all its elements and dimensions: faith, preparation for the sacrament, the rite, the profession of faith, incorporation into Christ and into the Church, ethical consequences, active participation in the life of the Church. The intimate connection between baptism, faith, and the Church must be emphasized. Only in this way does it become clear how marriage between baptized persons is a true sacrament *ex opere operato*, "by the very fact of the action's being performed" [see CCC 1128], that is to say, not because it is "automatic", but because of its intrinsic character.

III. Creation and Redemption

Marriage, Willed by God

Everything was created in Christ, by Christ, and for Christ. Hence, even though marriage was instituted by God the Creator, it becomes, nevertheless, a sign [see CCC 1617] of the mystery of the union of Christ the Bridegroom with the Church, his Bride, and it is in a certain way ordered to that mystery. This marriage, when it is celebrated between baptized persons, is elevated to the dignity of a sacrament, strictly speaking, and its meaning is then to make the couple participate in the spousal love of Christ and his Church.

Inseparability from the Work of Christ

In the case of two baptized persons, marriage as an institution willed by God the Creator is inseparable from the marriage sacrament. The sacramentality of a marriage of baptized persons is not an accidental quality, as though it were an optional accessory that could be added to the arrangement or not; it is inherent and essential to marriage, to such an extent that it cannot be separated from it.

Every Marriage of Baptized Persons Must Be Sacramental

It follows from the preceding propositions that, for the baptized, there can be no real, true conjugal state different from the one willed by Christ. In this sacrament the Christian man and woman, by giving themselves and accepting one another as spouses through their personal and free consent, are radically liberated from that "hardness of heart" of which Jesus spoke (see Mt 19:8). It actually becomes possible for them to live in an abiding love because, through the sacrament, they are really and truly taken up into the mystery of the spousal union of Christ and the Church. Hence the Church cannot, in any way, acknowledge that two baptized persons are in a conjugal state that is in conformity with their dignity as a "new creation in Christ", if they have not been joined by the sacrament of matrimony.

The "Lawful" Marriage of Non-Christians

The power and greatness of the grace of Christ extend to all men, even beyond the boundaries of the Church, by reason of the universality of the salvific will of God. They inform all human married love and confirm "created nature" and likewise marriage "as it was from the beginning" [Mt 19:8]. Men and women who have not yet been reached by the proclamation of the gospel are joined together through the human covenant of a lawful marriage. This covenant is provided with goods and authentic values that assure its soundness. But it is necessary to keep in mind that, even though the spouses may not be aware of it, these values come from God the Creator and are inscribed in a rudimentary form within the spousal love that unites Christ and the Church.

The Union of Christians Unaware of the Demands of Their Baptism

It would be contradictory, then, to say that Christians baptized in the Catholic Church can really and truly regress, settling for a non-sacramental marriage statute. That would be tantamount to thinking that they can be content with the "shadow" while Christ is offering them the "reality" of his spousal love.

Nevertheless, we cannot ignore cases in which the conscience of certain Christians has been deformed by ignorance or invincible error. These Christians end up believing, then, that they can enter into a true marriage and at the same time exclude the sacrament.

In this situation, they are incapable of contracting a valid sacramental marriage, since they deny the faith and do not have the intention of doing what the Church does. Yet, on the other hand, the natural right to enter into marriage does not therefore cease to exist. They are, then, capable of giving themselves and accepting one another as spouses by reason of their intention and of bringing about an irrevocable pact. This mutual and irrevocable giving creates a psychological relationship between them that differs, by its inner structure, from a relationship that is merely temporary.

Despite that, the relationship just described cannot in any way be recognized by the Church as a non-sacramental conjugal partnership, even though it presents the appearance of a marriage. Indeed, for the Church there is no such thing as a natural marriage between two baptized persons apart from the sacrament, but only a natural marriage elevated to the dignity of the sacrament.

"Gradual" Marriages

The previous considerations show the error and the danger of introducing or tolerating certain practices, consisting of the successive celebration, by the same couple, of various wedding ceremonies at different stages, even if they are in principle interconnected. Neither is it advisable to permit a priest or a deacon to attend, as clergymen, a non-sacramental marriage that a baptized couple pretend to celebrate, nor should they accompany the ceremony with their prayers.

Civil Marriage

In a pluralistic society, the authority of the state can demand that a couple comply with an official formality that makes their married state a matter of public record. It can also enact laws that establish in clear and correct terms the civil effects that derive from marriage, as well as familial duties and rights. It is necessary, however, to instruct the Catholic faithful adequately about the fact that this official formality, which is usually called civil marriage, does not constitute for them a true marriage. The only exceptions to this rule are (1) the case where there has been a dispensation from the ordinary canonical form and (2) in the event of a prolonged absence of the qualified witness of the Church, in which case civil marriage can serve as an extraordinary canonical form for the celebration of a sacramental marriage (see canon 1098 in the 1917 *Code of Canon Law* [7]). As far as it concerns non-Christians, and frequently, also, non-Catholics, this civil ceremony can have constitutive value, either for a lawful marriage or for a sacramental marriage.

IV. Indissolubility

The Principle

The tradition of the early Church, founded on the teaching of Christ and of the apostles, affirms the indissolubility of marriage, even in the case of adultery. This principle is imperative, despite a few passages that are difficult to interpret and some instances of indulgence with regard to persons who found themselves in very difficult situations. Besides, it is not easy to come to a definite conclusion as to the extent and frequency of these instances.

---

[7] Cardinal Medina is writing in 1978, and he cites the 1917 *Code of Canon Law*. The 1983 *Code of Canon Law*, in canon 1112, describes the procedure to be followed when no priest or deacon is available. Prior approval of the conference of bishops and permission of the Holy See is required before a diocesan bishop can delegate a lay person to assist at marriages where priests or deacons are lacking.

The Doctrine of the Church

The Council of Trent declared that the Church does not err when she has taught and teaches, according to evangelical and apostolic doctrine, that the marital bond cannot be broken because of adultery (DS 1807). However, the Council anathematized only those who deny the authority of the Church on this matter. The reasons for this reserve were certain doubts that have been expressed in the course of history (the opinions of Ambrosiaster, Catarinus, and Cajetan) and, on the other hand, certain perspectives that approach ecumenism. It cannot be affirmed, therefore, that the Council had the intention of solemnly defining the indissolubility of marriage as a truth of faith. We must, nevertheless, take into account the words pronounced by Pius XI, in *Casti Connubii*, when referring to this canon: "If therefore the Church has not erred and does not err in teaching this, and consequently it is certain that the bond of marriage cannot be loosed even on account of the sin of adultery, it is evident that all the other weaker excuses that can be, and are usually brought forward, are of no value whatsoever [and cannot be taken into consideration]" (cf. DS 1807).

Intrinsic Indissolubility

The intrinsic indissolubility of marriage can be considered under different aspects and can have various foundations.

The problem can be considered from the spouses' point of view. Then we will say that the intimate union of marriage—the mutual self-giving of two persons—and conjugal love itself, as well as the good of the children, demand the indissoluble unity of said persons. From this is derived, for the spouses, the moral obligation to protect their marital covenant, to preserve it, and to develop it.

But marriage should be viewed also from God's perspective. The human act by which the spouses give themselves and receive one another, creates a bond that is founded in the will of God. This bond is inscribed on the creative act itself and eludes the will of men. It does not depend on the spouses' authority, and, as such, it is intrinsically indissoluble.

Viewed from a christological perspective, the indissolubility of Christian marriage ultimately has an even more profound basis, consisting of the fact that it is the image, the sacrament, and the witness of the indissoluble union between Christ and his Church. This is what has been called "the good of the sacrament". In this sense, indissolubility becomes a grace-filled event.

Perspectives of a social nature, also, are the basis for this indissolubility, something that is required by the institution itself. The personal decision of the spouses is assumed, protected, and strengthened by society, above all by the ecclesial community. Hence there is a commitment to the good of the children and to the common good. This is the ecclesial-juridical dimension of marriage.

All of these different aspects are closely interconnected. The fidelity to which the spouses are obligated must be protected by society, which is the Church. It is demanded by God the Creator as well as by Christ, who makes it possible by the outpouring of his grace.

Extrinsic Indissolubility and the Authority
of the Church on Marriage

In parallel to her praxis, the Church has elaborated a doctrine concerning her own authority in the field of marriage. In so doing, she has specified the extent and limits of that authority. The Church claims no authority whatsoever to dissolve a ratified and consummated sacramental marriage (*ratum et consummatum*). On account of very serious reasons, for the good of the faith and the salvation of souls, other kinds of marriages can be dissolved by the competent ecclesiastical authority or, according to another interpretation, be declared dissolved per se.

This teaching is only one particular case in the general theory of how Christian doctrine evolves in the Church. Today, this teaching is almost universally accepted by Catholic theologians.

This does not exclude, however, the possibility that the Church could specify in even greater detail the concepts of sacramentality and consummation [of a marriage]. In that case, the Church would explain even more clearly the meaning of these concepts. In that way, the whole ensemble of doctrine concerning the indissolubility of marriage could be proposed in a more profound and more precise synthesis.

V. Those Who Are Divorced and Remarried

The Gospel's Radicalism

Faithful to the radicalism of the gospel, the Church cannot address her faithful in any language other than that of Saint Paul's: "To the married I give charge, not I but the Lord, that the wife should not separate from her husband (but if she does, let her remain single or else be reconciled to her husband)—and that the husband should not divorce his wife" (1 Cor 7:10–11). From this it follows that any new union subsequent to a divorce obtained according to civil law is neither a regular union nor legitimate.

Prophetic Testimony

This strictness is not derived from a purely disciplinary law or from a certain legalism. It is based upon the judgment that the Lord himself passed on the matter (Mk 10:6ff.). So understood, this severe law is a prophetic testimony given concerning the definitive faithfulness of the love that joins Christ with the Church, demonstrating at the same time that the love of spouses is taken up into Christ's own charity (Eph 5:23–32).

Being Away from the Sacraments

This incompatibility between the [civil] statute concerning the "divorced and remarried" and the precept and mystery of the paschal love of the Lord makes it impossible for them to receive, in the Holy Eucharist, the sign of that union with Christ. Their return to Eucharistic Communion must be by way of penance, which means "sorrow and hatred for the sin committed and the firm purpose not to sin again" (Council of Trent, DS 1676). All Christians must remember the words of the Apostle: "Whoever, therefore, eats the bread or drinks the cup of the Lord in an unworthy manner will be guilty of profaning the body and blood of the Lord. Let a man examine himself, and so eat of the bread and drink of the cup. For any one who eats and drinks without discerning the body eats and drinks judgment upon himself" (1 Cor 11:27–29).

Pastoral Care of the Divorced and Remarried

This unlawful situation does not permit these persons to live in full communion with the Church. Yet Christians who find themselves in this situation are not excluded from the action of God's grace or from a bond with the Church. They should not be deprived of pastoral care (see the Papal Address of Paul VI, November 4, 1977, in *Documentation Catholique*, no. 1012). Numerous obligations that proceed from Christian baptism continue to be in force, even for them. They must watch over the religious formation of their children. Christian prayer, public as well as private, penance, and certain apostolic activities continue to be for them pathways of Christian life. They should not be rejected but helped, as should be all Christians who, with the help of Christ's grace, are making an effort to free themselves from sin.

Combating the Reasons for Divorce

Every day it becomes more imperative to develop pastoral action aimed at avoiding the proliferation of divorce and of new civil unions of divorced persons. We must instill especially in those who are preparing for marriage a vivid awareness of all their future responsibilities as spouses and parents. It is important to present in an ever more effective form the authentic meaning of sacramental marriage as a covenant realized "in the Lord" (1 Cor 7:39). In this way, Christians will find themselves better prepared to keep the commandment of the Lord and to give witness to the union of Christ with his Church. Furthermore, this would be for the greater good of spouses, of children, and of society itself.

PART TWO

"BE FRUITFUL AND MULTIPLY"

(Genesis 1:28)

CHAPTER THREE

The Family: A Religious Entity

I. Introduction

The family, being a human reality, has multiple dimensions. They are all so intertwined that it is not possible to detach completely one from the others: it is the complexity typical of humanity, an expression both of its richness and of its limitations. Furthermore, each facet of a human being can be fully understood only in relation to the other aspects, each one adding its own complement to the whole, just as each cut of a gem contributes to the vivid brilliance of the whole precious stone. Only God, who is a pure and most perfect spirit, possesses incomparable beauty and glory in his simplicity, but even then Christian faith teaches us that in the unity of God there are three personal relationships—the Father, the Son, and the Holy Spirit—that express the richness of the Divine Being.

It would be unrealistic to reduce the family to a one-dimensional unit, or to limit oneself to considering a single aspect of it. A holistic approach to the reality of the family implies viewing it from various angles: its history, its components or social conditions, its psychological elements, its biological factors, its cultural environment, its legal and economic framework, the moral precepts that govern it, and, finally,

This essay, dated February 1994, was composed before the publication of the "Letter to Families" by Pope John Paul II— ED.

its religious meaning. Yet it is a legitimate question whether there is one all-encompassing point of view that, without neglecting or in any way minimizing the other dimensions, provides the possibility of integrating them all within a vision that allows us to prioritize values and to establish the relative positions of those that are of secondary importance. This brief essay attempts to answer this question.

II. The Religious Dimension: The Essential Element in Man

Man cannot be fully understood except in his total and permanent relation to God. When the Apostle Paul said "we live to the Lord" (Rom 14:8), he was affirming exactly the same thing that Peter had said to Jesus years before, at a moment when many of those who had until then been his disciples were abandoning him. When Jesus asked the apostles whether they too would abandon him, Peter replied, "Lord, to whom shall we go? You have the words of eternal life" (Jn 6:68). It is the same idea Saint Augustine expressed so beautifully in his book *Confessions* when he wrote "You, Lord, have made us for yourself, and our hearts are restless until they rest in you."

Man is related to God in multiple ways—all of them intertwined, all of them bringing joy—and all of them serve as material for man's prayer life and nourish his moral development.

We have with God a relationship of origin: he is our Creator, the beginning and cause of our existence. Without his creative will, we simply would not exist. Not only did he create us initially, but he also sustains our existence from moment to moment, in such a way that we can say we are a "continuing creation".

We have with God a relationship of life: he has given us life, and has given it to us at various levels—physical life, biological life, cultural, working, intellectual life, and, finally, participation in his own life, in the capacity of adopted children destined for the inheritance of heaven.

We have with God a relationship of purpose: he is our final destination and our definitive happiness. If we do not attain the possession and love of him, the meaning of our existence will have been frustrated.

We have with God a relationship of salvation: being sinners, and at the same time having offended God and destroyed our own dignity, we know that he alone could stretch out to us his saving hand, and he did so by sending us his Son, Jesus Christ, in order to lead us back to him.

These relationships with God are not something "added on" to our being, to our nature; they are part of our human condition and therefore belong to every man, to those who are aware of these bonds as well as to those who do not know about them. There are not two kinds of humanity, but only one; there are not two ultimate purposes for man, but only one.

It is a misfortune for a man not to know that he has a relationship with God that cannot be lost; it is worse still to reject it. Someone who does not know these bonds, which are cords of love that sustain him in relation to God, does not perceive the meaning of his life, cannot live in the joy of knowing what he is here on earth for and what is the final and definitive destiny of his existence.

The preceding enables us to see clearly that the "religious dimension" is not the sole property of the ordained ministers of the Church or of persons consecrated to a life of celibate chastity, but it belongs to every Christian, indeed, to every man. I think that there are some Christians who believe, or at least act, as though their bonds with God were of an inferior quality to those of priests, deacons, or religious, and that they can be content with a more or less occasional relationship with God; they imagine that it is not their lot to be always and necessarily related to him, at every moment and in every action. Perhaps it is not expressed in so many words, but certain attitudes cannot be explained except as a consequence of this thought. In any case, thinking this way would be like dividing up the requirements of the First Commandment of the law of God, "and you shall love the LORD your God with all your heart, and with all your soul, and with all your might" (Deut 6:4; Mt 22:37; Lk 10:27), as if this basic precept applied in its entirety to clerics and religious, and only to a lesser degree to laymen as they live and work in their various situations. Neither the biblical text nor the way the Church has always understood it authorizes us to divide the First Commandment into different requirements that are more or less obligatory. The gospel did not set up two levels of morality, nor did Saint Paul ever authorize such a thing. The New Testament is a message directed to all disciples of Christ, and the teaching of the Second Vatican Council about the vocation or universal call to sanctity (LG, chap. 5) delineates in very precise form a conviction that belongs to the most authentic spiritual tradition of the Church.

Having said this, it is clear that within man there are no "gospel-free, autonomous zones" or areas that are morally "indifferent"; every human act necessarily has a plus or a minus sign in the relationship with God. Thus, "religiosity" is not simply a set of devotional practices—which are in themselves something good—but rather the permanent and conscious attitude of the Christian who views each one of his acts from the perspective of his relationship with God.

THE FAMILY: A RELIGIOUS ENTITY

One very essential component of religiosity is the desire to direct all of one's actions to the honor of God, not only those that pertain to liturgical worship or various forms of piety, but every act of desiring or not desiring. That is what Saint Ignatius of Loyola stresses in the "Principle and Foundation" of his famous *Spiritual Exercises*, when he says that "man was created to praise, reverence, and serve the Lord our God, and thereby to save his soul, and all other things on the face of the earth were created for man, in order to help him in pursuing the end for which he was created. Hence it follows that man has to make use of them to the extent that they help him toward his goal, and must also detach himself from them to the extent that they hinder him [from reaching his goal]." When Saint Ignatius wrote this he was not thinking only about the Jesuits but about every Christian, whether a clergyman or religious of the Church or a layman.

The preceding reflections lead us to affirm, or reaffirm, that the religious dimension is the structural principle or, to put it in a different way, the "spinal column" of human life.

III. Marriage, an Intrinsically Religious Reality

Sacred Scripture teaches us that God created the human being as male and female so that they would be equal, in spite of the differences between them, capable of loving and helping one another, and of procreating children through the physical expression of love (see Gen 1:26–27; 2:18, 21–24). The union of man and woman, as the Bible presents it, is not casual or temporary but so powerful that it must take precedence even over paternal or filial relations within a family. "Therefore a man leaves his father and his mother and cleaves to his wife, and they become one flesh" (Gen 2:24). "What therefore God has joined together, let no man put asunder" (Mt 19:6; Mk 10:9). If all human life has its origin in God's loving design, it is fair to say that marriage bears in a special way the stamp of God's action. It is even possible to see in the diversity of the persons who make up a family an "echo" or "image" of the Divine Persons who are God one and triune.

It is no mere coincidence that in Sacred Scripture the relationship of God with his people is described by means of the image of a nuptial love (Song; Hos 2; Ezek 16; Rev 21). Along this same line it is natural that the Apostle Paul takes the relationship of Christ, the Bridegroom, with the Church, his Bride, as a model and pattern for the love between married Christians. "Husbands, love your wives, as Christ loved the church and gave himself up for her, that he might sanctify her. . . . This is a great mystery, and I mean in reference to Christ and the *church*" (Eph 5:25–26, 32, emphasis added). Marital fidelity is patterned on that of Christ for his Church; the fruitfulness of the Christian home has Holy Mother Church as its model and participates in her spiritual character. It is important for married Christians to ask themselves the following questions: Do I love my spouse with a heart so disposed that it may be a reflection of the Heart of Christ? Do I think about my duty to be for my spouse a support in his sanctification, in her search for God? Do I make an effort to purify my love for my spouse, so that the traces of selfishness will disappear?

If we asked some Christian couples why they are going to be married, it is quite possible that we would get many different answers, with varying degrees of precision, but would there be many who would declare that they are getting married to serve God in the state of matrimony, to help each other find God, to bring into this world children of God to love him, praise him, and serve him? Yet these are the proper ends of a marriage that is contracted in the light of that admirable nuptial mystery of the salvific love of Christ for the Church.

When marriage is viewed thus—and it is the only way of looking at it if one sees it in terms of the faith—we will be far from examining it through the prism of the superficialities and conventional trappings that oftentimes surround the celebration of this sacrament. The celebration of marriage ought to be an act marked in every sense by a deeply religious stamp, since it is nothing other than the mutual offering of the spouses themselves, who present to God their willingness to love each other as Christ loved the Church.

We must make a clarification here: when we speak of marriage, we are referring to the sacramental union that joins two Christians indissolubly for a lifetime or else to the natural union that can exist between those who are not Christians. A living arrangement between two Christians who are not joined by the sacrament is not a true marriage because for Christians there is no marriage which is not sacramental. It is not lawful for Christians to content themselves with a union sanctioned only by civil law. If both are single, that would be living together in the sin of fornication; if one has already been married in the Church to a third person, that would be adulterous cohabitation. These unions in sin are certainly not a reflection of the sanctifying love that unites Christ with the Church! It is sad to have to say it so plainly, and some will think that it is very harsh to put it this way; the truth is, nevertheless, that this is the doctrine of the Church, founded on the gospel, and that the truth makes us truly free (Jn 8:32).

IV. The Family, a Religious Reality

The Christian family is born of sacramental marriage. For those who are not Christians there exists a familial reality that is also religious, that originates in their natural, non-sacramental marriage. A Christian family is born, then, from an act of grace: the sacrament of matrimony. Its ultimate purpose is guiding all the members of the family toward God, above all, the group that is sometimes called the "nuclear" family—the spouses and their children—but also other persons who in various ways are integrated in the family community. God cannot be absent from the awareness of a Christian family; if everyone knows that he was there at the start of the family community and that the family is journeying to him, it follows that God is going to be present in an explicit way in the life of that family.

The first way of acknowledging the presence of God in the home is prayer. Not only individual prayer but also the prayer of the whole family unit. It can take many forms: the reading of Sacred Scripture, the Holy Rosary, prayer before meals, especially before that meal at which the greater part of the family members are gathered, the month of Mary, novenas such as that of Christmas, and so on.

An important way is the presence of sacred images in the family dwelling: the crucifix, the image of the Sacred Heart, a picture of the Blessed Virgin Mary under one of her titles, or of some saint to whom the family has a special devotion, such as Saint Teresa of the Andes, or the Blessed Laurita Vicuña. We should not abandon the beautiful custom of placing the image of the Sacred Heart of Jesus at the doors of our houses or the practice of setting up a family altar in a prominent place in the home.

The parents of the family must be the first to proclaim the

gospel to their children. Christian parents must be aware that, in order to carry out their duties, it is not enough to provide for the material welfare and education of their children; they must communicate to them, by word and by their example, the Christian and Catholic faith. A Christian father or mother must put aside the fear of speaking about God to their children; to teach them and correct them, they should use arguments and examples taken from Sacred Scripture, especially the Gospels. And when the time comes for the children or adolescents to receive the sacraments of First Communion and confirmation, it is expected of Christian parents that they be involved in the catechetical programs of the parish and assume their responsibilities to support and guide their children.

A very special moment of God's presence in the family is the participation of family members in the Sunday Mass of their parish, chapel, or nearby church. If Sunday Mass is the center of the life of the Church, as the Second Vatican Council teaches, what are we to think about the fact that there are Christian parents who content themselves with "sending" their children to Mass, without giving them the example of their own conviction and interest by participating in the Mass every Sunday, without excusing themselves, unless there is a truly important reason? On the contrary, when children see in their parents an interest and a concern about fulfilling their religious duties and a devotion to the act of worship that is central to the Catholic faith, they themselves feel supported and motivated to participate in the Holy Mass.

As with all other realities and areas of human life, the family acquires its full meaning only when it is understood and lived in a religious way. In Christian terms, the family is the fundamental cell of the Church. Permeated with the faith and nourished by the faith, the family founded on the sacred sacramental bond between the spouses is, in all truth, a "domestic Church".

There are, sometimes, between Christians, irregular and unlawful unions that are not marriage but that give rise to natural bonds that oblige the parties morally. These unions cannot become entirely like Christian families, but we must consider that they constitute a "de facto" framework that, on the one hand, cannot be recognized as lawful or accepted as such, but that, on the other hand, gives rise to religious duties. This is not the time to discuss in detail these situations, which are sometimes extremely painful and run quite a wide gamut of variant forms. Some sort of pastoral care cannot be denied them, but the utmost care should be taken, for the sake of fidelity to the truth, not to confuse something that is not a lawful marriage with something that is.[1] Charity

---

[1] On this subject the Apostolic Exhortation *Familiaris Consortio* noted:

"Daily experience unfortunately shows that people who have obtained a divorce usually intend to enter into a new union, obviously not with a Catholic religious ceremony. Since this is an evil that, like the others, is affecting more and more Catholics as well, the problem must be faced with resolution and without delay. The Synod Fathers studied it expressly. The Church, which was set up to lead to salvation all people and especially the baptized, cannot abandon to their own devices those who have been previously bound by sacramental marriage and who have attempted a second marriage. The Church will therefore make untiring efforts to put at their disposal her means of salvation.

"Pastors must know that, for the sake of truth, they are obliged to exercise careful discernment of situations. There is in fact a difference between those who have sincerely tried to save their first marriage and have been unjustly abandoned, and those who through their own grave fault have destroyed a canonically valid marriage. Finally, there are those who have entered into a second union for the sake of the children's upbringing, and who are sometimes subjectively certain in conscience that their previous and irreparably destroyed marriage had never been valid.

"Together with the Synod, I earnestly call upon pastors and the whole community of the faithful to help the divorced, and with solicitous care to make sure that they do not consider themselves as separated from the Church, for as baptized persons they can, and indeed must, share in her life. They

cannot be practiced at the expense of the truth, for then it would cease to be true charity. Jesus said, "What therefore God has joined together, let no man put asunder" (Mt 19:6):

---

should be encouraged to listen to the word of God, to attend the Sacrifice of the Mass, to persevere in prayer, to contribute to works of charity and to community efforts in favor of justice, to bring up their children in the Christian faith, to cultivate the spirit and practice of penance and thus implore, day by day, God's grace. Let the Church pray for them, encourage them and show herself a merciful mother, and thus sustain them in faith and hope.

"However, the Church reaffirms her practice, which is based upon Sacred Scripture, of not admitting to Eucharistic Communion divorced persons who have remarried. They are unable to be admitted thereto from the fact that their state and condition of life objectively contradict that union of love between Christ and the Church which is signified and effected by the Eucharist. Besides this, there is another special pastoral reason: if these people were admitted to the Eucharist, the faithful would be led into error and confusion regarding the Church's teaching about the indissolubility of marriage.

"Reconciliation in the sacrament of Penance, which would open the way to the Eucharist, can only be granted to those who, repenting of having broken the sign of the Covenant and of fidelity to Christ, are sincerely ready to undertake a way of life that is no longer in contradiction to the indissolubility of marriage. This means, in practice, that when, for serious reasons, such as for example the children's upbringing, a man and a woman cannot satisfy the obligation to separate, they 'take on themselves the duty to live in complete continence, that is, by abstinence from the acts proper to married couples.'

"Similarly, the respect due to the sacrament of Matrimony, to the couples themselves and their families, and also to the community of the faithful, forbids any pastor, for whatever reason or pretext even of a pastoral nature, to perform ceremonies of any kind for divorced people who remarry. Such ceremonies would give the impression of the celebration of a new sacramentally valid marriage, and would thus lead people into error concerning the indissolubility of a validly contracted marriage.

"By acting in this way, the Church professes her own fidelity to Christ and to His truth. At the same time she shows motherly concern for these children of hers, especially those who, through no fault of their own, have been abandoned by their legitimate partner.

"With firm confidence she believes that those who have rejected the Lord's command and are still living in this state will be able to obtain from God the grace of conversion and salvation, provided that they have persevered in prayer, penance and charity" (no. 84).— ED.

let no one ask the Church to claim for herself a power that Christ has not conferred upon her by calling "all right" something that is not right in the eyes of God.

V. The Family, the Domestic Church

It is very appropriate to conclude by recalling what the *Catechism of the Catholic Church* says about the family as a "domestic Church": this is precisely the subtitle that introduces the last numbers of the article devoted to the sacrament of marriage:

> 1655. Christ chose to be born and grow up in the bosom of the holy family of Joseph and Mary. The Church is nothing other than "the family of God." From the beginning, the core of the Church was often constituted by those who had become believers "together with all [their] household" (cf. Acts 18:8). When they were converted, they desired that "their whole household" should also be saved (cf. Acts 16:31; Acts 11:14). These families who became believers were islands of Christian life in an unbelieving world.

> 1656. In our own time, in a world often alien and even hostile to faith, believing families are of primary importance as centers of living, radiant faith. For this reason the Second Vatican Council, using an ancient expression, calls the family *Ecclesia domestica* (LG 11; cf. FC 21). It is in the bosom of the family that parents are "by word and example . . . the first heralds of the faith with regard to their children. They should encourage them in the vocation which is proper to each child, fostering with special care any religious vocation" (LG 11).

> 1657. It is here that the father of the family, the mother, children, and all members of the family exercise the *priesthood*

of the baptized in a privileged way "by the reception of the sacraments, prayer and thanksgiving, the witness of a holy life, and self-denial and active charity" (LG 10). Thus the home is the first school of Christian life and "a school for human enrichment" (GS 52 § 1). Here one learns endurance and the joy of work, fraternal love, generous—even repeated—forgiveness, and above all divine worship in prayer and the offering of one's life.

How encouraging it is, the Christian and Catholic teaching on marriage and the family!

CHAPTER FOUR

The Indissolubility of Marriage: Guarantor of True Dignity

An Interview Conducted by
Christiane Raczynski

What is marriage? The pen of Don Andrés Bello did not waver when the illustrious jurist, in composing our [Chilean] Civil Code, wrote: "Marriage is a solemn contract by which a man and a woman join together for the present and indissolubly for the rest of their lives, in order to live together, to procreate, and to help one another."

It would not have been as easy for him to write this in 1994, the International Year of the Family, proclaimed by the United Nations and endorsed by churches throughout the world. The family presently finds itself at the center of heated debates, because there are new concepts of marriage. Some argue that other equivalent types of associations exist. Others, that the indissolubility of marriage stipulated in our code of law is a "confessional" ["denominational"] understanding of marriage, a view which is hardly "pluralist" and therefore inadequate for today's world.

This interview [with then-Archbishop Jorge Medina Estévez], conducted by Christiane Raczynski, appeared in *El Mercurio*, April 17, 1994, section E, page 10.

Even though the *Catechism of the Catholic Church* reaffirms the indissolubility of marriage, there are also increasing doubts among Catholics with respect to this subject. Archbishop Jorge Medina, a member of the Pontifical Council for the Family, an institution created by Pope John Paul II to strengthen the basic cell of society, has answered some of the most frequently-asked questions on the subject.

*You have just attended the final session convened by
the Pontifical Council on the Family in Rome, in
which an analysis was made of the present state of this
institution. What was the diagnosis?*

The Pontifical Council for the Family is an institution created by the present Pontiff, and the scope of its responsibilities is rather broad. It deals with issues concerning the family, youth, and marriage; it is rather difficult to give a precise job description. Its president is currently Cardinal Alfonso López Trujillo, from Colombia, formerly archbishop of Medellín. At the plenary session we evaluate the situation of the family, and especially that of women, in today's world. The role of this Council is to furnish materials to the permanent body, which carries on the particular work of the institution throughout the year, following the guidelines of the Holy Father's "Letter to Families"; it also has the task of initiating further discussion of the papal document *Familiaris Consortio*, which is one of the bases of our work.

How is the family threatened today?

The family faces threats from many quarters. The statistics published recently in many countries show that its stability is seriously compromised. In addition to this problem there are other situations, for example, that of the working woman who has to be away from home, and the undeniable repercussions this has on the children. That was an issue we considered with great care. We also analyzed the pressure that is exerted on the family in many parts of the world to limit births by whatever means. The Holy Father has just sent a severe letter to Dr. Nafis Sadik, a Pakistani woman and physician, who plans to recommend, at the world population conference that will take place in Cairo in October [1994], a universal acceptance of contraceptive methods. Among them she includes abortion, which is not a contraceptive, since the procedure is carried out after conception has occurred. All the presidents of the Latin American episcopal conferences gathered in Celam also sent a severe warning to Dr. Sadik for the same reason.

There is a tendency today to disassociate marriage from the family, sexuality from procreation. In your judgment, what are the consequences of this?

Man is a unity, and that oneness is not something external to him, nor the result of an imposition of positive law, but rather the result of his nature. Concepts and realities such as marriage–family, sexuality–procreation, must necessarily be viewed from the perspective of this unity of man and of his destiny. It is essential that we have clarity in our thinking about the unity of the human being. If this clarity does not exist, certitudes are watered down and everything ends up being debatable, a matter of opinion. One very negative sign is the fact that in certain circles of the United Nations they cannot manage to define what the family is, or else they avoid the concept of marriage.

Another example, I would say almost colorful if it were

not so tragic, is the recommendation by the European Parliament that children be given in adoption to homosexual couples. The tragic thing here is that there is no concept of what a family is. The Pope begins his "Letter to Families" by saying that the family is founded upon marriage. This is the basis of the family. The family is made up of spouses, not of cohabiting persons. A family is constituted by persons who have united with one another, for the present and indissolubly and for the rest of their lives, in order to live together, to procreate, and to help one other. That is what a family is. In its wider meaning we can also include in it grandparents, grandchildren, and so on. It is a very rich circle.

But where does it come from, this tendency to separate these themes, to fragment them?

As a matter of fact, the delegated married couple from Chile who attended the Council for the Family, Señor and Señora Munzenmayer, pointed out what you are suggesting: that there is a policy aimed at separating God from the world, separating fertility from family, sexuality from marriage. This sort of division is leading us to what could be called a condition of moral schizophrenia, with fatal consequences for society.

I think that the deepest root is found in the separation of man from God. Man is not recognized as a work of God, as a being whose existence and reality emanate from a divine will; as a being, the only being—as the Pope insistently repeats—whom God has willed for his own sake. In current thought, a human being is not willed by God. He is just someone who appeared [on earth] without anyone knowing why or wherefore. And things that come into being by chance are not very important.

Man has forgotten that he is a creature of God, and he has forgotten about God. And when the one, living, and true God is forgotten, the human being begins to adore a series of idols: power, money, sexuality, which cease to be relative things and are turned into absolutes.

One of the arguments of those who favor this initiative is that someone who does not share the beliefs of Catholics cannot be obliged to maintain a regimen of indissolubility in marriage, because that runs counter to a "sound pluralism".

The indissolubility of marriage is demanded, not only by the Christian and Catholic faith, but by human nature itself. Only indissolubility guarantees the true equality and dignity of the man and the woman. Only indissolubility obligates one to take the marital commitment seriously. Only indissolubility provides a foundation for the stability of marriage. Only indissolubility makes unselfish fertility and procreation possible. Only indissolubility makes the radical demand to give oneself completely to the other spouse. Only indissolubility can curb inconstancy and escapades. Only indissolubility creates a favorable climate for bringing up children. Only indissolubility authenticates love, which intrinsically demands that it be "forever". Only indissolubility allows the spouses to give themselves to one another without reservations and without calculations. Only indissolubility can protect the nobility of conjugal love against the temptation to "use the other". Only indissolubility is a firm invitation to overcome crises, to forgive, and to arrive at the sacrificial maturity of love.

And all of this is implied by and undergirds the famous definition of marriage that appears in our Civil Code—a non-denominational document—drawn up by Don Andrés Bello: "Marriage is a solemn contract by which a man and a woman join together for the present and indissolubly for the rest of their lives, in order to live together, to procreate, and to help one another." Of course, indissolubility is not an absolute guarantee with regard to what can happen, but it is nevertheless a value that constitutes the foundation on which true marital consent is based, and if this foundation is lacking, there is no marriage to speak of. If the day comes when a divorce law is introduced in Chile, the moment will have arrived to modify the definition of marriage given in the Civil Code. Should that ever happen, it would be simpler to say that the government has put an end to the institution of marriage and replaced it with other sorts of contracts. Legitimate? Moral? No.

When the Bible explains that God created man and woman, Adam says, "This is flesh of my flesh and bone of my bones." What is flesh of my flesh is something so very mine that it cannot be another's; it can no longer cease being mine. The meaning of the biblical words is obvious. And when the Bible says, "let no man separate what God has joined together", it is speaking, not about a positive law, but about human nature itself. The Pope, furthermore, says this in his "Letter to Families".

What, then, does true pluralism consist of, with regard to this issue?

The word "pluralism" is a rather complex term. There can be pluralism in matters of art, for example. The baroque and neoclassical styles are valid artistic forms. There is no unique canon or one single truth in art, but when we enter the realm of human nature, it is not pluralism to allow what is contrary to it. With regard to this issue it has also been argued that in ancient times, under the Mosaic law, divorce was permitted. I do not interpret this as a form of pluralism, but rather within the framework of a gradual understanding of moral demands. Slavery, too, existed in the Old Covenant and in the New, but the fact that there was slavery for many centuries would not be a reason to say that slavery is not contrary to the natural law and that, therefore, we could have slaves today.

Another argument advanced [in support of divorce] is
freedom of conscience.

Conscience must be well formed. A person can have an invincibly erroneous conscience and by dint of that may commit acts for which he is not culpable, because he does not realize and does not perceive that they are bad. That does not mean that this person is excused from seeking the truth. It certainly does not mean that he can demand that the law that governs society should sanction what is not in conformity with the natural law. Society can tolerate some things, but to tolerate does not mean to approve or to give them the status of legitimacy. Houses of prostitution are called [in Spanish] "houses of tolerance". This does not mean that society approves of them and says that this is all right and that they deserve the same *status* as other legitimate activities. It is tolerated because nothing more can be done about it.

Could it be said that the [civil] annulments of the
sort which are granted today [in Chile] are another
"institution of tolerance"?

I think that they could be classified as such. I know they are a fraud, but that being the case, they have one advantage over divorce: whoever resorts to it knows that he or she is lying and causing others to lie. He knows that he has entered the realm of falsehood, and this seems to me less harmful than to have recourse to an eventual divorce law that "leaves you with a clear conscience" because you have "complied" with the law—with a human law that contravenes the law of God. Whereas in the "fraudulent annulments" the toleration is evident, divorce legitimizes what is not legitimate.

You say that indissolubility is based on natural law.
What, then, is the role of the sacrament?

The sacrament elevates marriage so that it becomes a sign of grace, but the sacrament rests on the natural institution of marriage. For those who are married in the Church, this is one more reason, in addition to the natural indissolubility, since for two Christians who contract marriage, their union is a symbol, an image of the love with which Christ loved and loves his Church. This constitutes a very deep, very profound vision [of marriage], but this is not the only reason for its indissolubility. If Scripture took marriage as the model of the love God has for his people, or the love Christ has for his Church, it is because the human love was already indissoluble.

The importance of natural law stands out here.
However, modern man has enormous difficulties in
recognizing that this law is imprinted in his very
nature. What cultural factors today prevent people from
acknowledging the natural law?

There is now the influence of a relativist mentality, which the Pope deals with at length in his encyclical *Veritatis splendor.*

Morality has ceased to be a set of objective values, independent of what may happen [that is, the consequences of an act]. Today, instead of judging consequences with reference to morality, they have constructed a morality based on outcomes. This relativism is expressed, for example, when people behave contrary to the virtue of chastity, arguing that they have to adapt to the changing culture. In other words, morality is being transformed into a result of or a response to statistics. Whatever happens numerically is what we have to live with. If we take this stance, we are abandoning any objective parameters for deciding what is right and what is wrong.

This involves applying to morality the criteria of the empirical sciences, of technology, while forgetting the common good.

It appears to me that there is an analogy between the two approaches. But the central ingredient here is the fact that God is forgotten. When a person does not believe in God, he is left without one of the pillars upon which absolute value judgments are set. Everything then becomes more or less debatable, relative. Consequently, the word "sin" disappears; all "behaviors" are equivalent, in practice; thus, to be married to a lawful wife is, practically speaking, the same as "living together", or else having relations with a woman whom one does not intend to marry is considered the equivalent of marital relations with one's wife. All of this is covered up with the cloak of that magic word "maturity" [*madurez*]. Who knows what meaning they are attributing to it.

The common good has been defined as the set of conditions that enable persons and groups to reach their own fulfillment. "Fulfillment" is not only an external social order [relative to the persons or groups], but that spiritual disposition that places man on the road toward his ultimate goal and final destiny. If we keep *this* in mind, it becomes clear that not just any technical possibility is in itself moral, or conducive to the common good. What threatens the fulfillment of man is incompatible with the common good.

What would you say to your own Catholic faithful,
who feel paralyzed when they are accused of turning
something based on their own beliefs into a universal
law?

They should not be afraid, because if a Catholic or a non-Catholic stands up and defends the indissolubility of marriage, he is performing a great service for everyone else. A marriage that is indissoluble is an immense service to man and to woman; the dissolution of marriage through divorce is for a great number of women the beginning of a lamentable fate.

Positive law has to conform to natural law? Why is
that?

Positive law has to agree with natural law. When positive law contradicts natural law, in the eyes of the Church, it is not a law at all. This is not my own opinion, but the teaching found throughout the *Catechism of the Catholic Church*, which is the authentic point of reference with respect to the doctrine of the Church. The reason for it is that positive law is derived from the eternal law and the natural law. Positive law is not self-justifying. Saint Thomas Aquinas says that it is a "rational ordinance", that is to say, a code of laws in conformity with reason and consequently with the truth, and he adds that it is promulgated "with a view to the common good". So a positive law that did not conform to reason and to the truth, and did not contribute to the common good, would not be a law. A human legislator must always take care that his legislation is in keeping with the truth and is directed toward the common good.

Some maintain, however, that human law has to take up a position between the demands of the ideal and what is possible.

No doubt there are tragic situations, including some which we could even call quite dramatic. But I do not think that the way to solve these problems is to destroy the natural law. If unfortunate situations arise, some way of diminishing the disadvantages has to be found, but under no circumstances can one attribute a perfectly legitimate status to something that is not in line with the natural law and with the law of God. It is one thing to find palliative measures for situations that have no perfect solution, but it is quite another to accept the establishment of a solution contrary to the natural law, as though it were equivalent to the natural law.

Marriage is a reality that does not have its origin in the state. So, can the state determine what its end should be?

The institution of marriage is certainly prior to the state. Man appeared on earth perhaps five hundred thousand years ago, and the state as such probably made its appearance ten thousand years ago. Historically, marriage and the family are earlier institutions than the state. The Pope says in his "Letter to Families" that the family has a certain sovereignty. Therefore I think that, when the state legislates well, it will do so recognizing, accepting, and reinforcing the natural institution of marriage. When the state passes laws that weaken the institution of marriage, it is arrogating for itself a right that it does not have.

Our political constitution [in Chile] guarantees, as one of its founding principles, that man is prior and superior to the state, and hence that his fundamental rights are "acknowledged" and not "granted" by the state. Even if we were to assume, hypothetically, that a law on divorce were approved, that law would violate the conscience of all those who married under the system of indissolubility, since it would be changing the rules of the game. It is not enough to say, "Don't get a divorce if you don't want one", because together with that you are also saying, "If you want, you can get a divorce." And that was not their will or what they had consented to. It is as if you were to change the definition of property rights. It currently means that you may use, enjoy, and dispose of a thing, provided that it is done in a manner not contrary to law or against someone else's rights. Now if you add that property rights last five days, we are talking about something different, and we should therefore change its name. It is no longer what the legislator defined as property.

Today in our country divorce is proposed as a remedy for certain irreparable situations.

If it is passed to "remedy" some situations, it will be opening the door to the sole ground that proves in the long run to be real: divorce by mutual consent. If legislation has stipulated fifteen possible grounds for divorce, people will go for the simplest one. So if two persons are in agreement, they can fabricate proof for the easiest grounds, and thus they end up in that same fraudulent situation of the notorious "civil annulments" that people talk about so much. By another route we will arrive, practically speaking, at the same destination.

Then what can be done in those irreparable situations?

This problem, which is difficult and extremely painful, involves many variables. From a Christian perspective one has to say that there are situations in which the Cross of Christ is made present very forcefully. And if I am not willing to embrace the Cross of Christ, which has different dimensions, I cannot say that I am a Christian. Whoever wants to be my disciple, says Jesus, let him take up his cross daily and follow me [Lk 9:23]. Elsewhere, the Apostle Paul says, "For many, of whom I tell you even with tears, live as enemies of the cross of Christ" [Phil 3:18]. We have to take up the cross; if we do not, we simply cannot be Christians. To take up the cross demands a great deal of effort and, many times, heroism. During the great persecutions of the Christian faith in the first centuries of the Church, or in Mexico in this [the twentieth] century, there were people who faced the alternative of renouncing their faith or giving up their lives, and they preferred to give up their lives, because they realized that faith is an unrenounceable value, which cannot be compared with any other value whatsoever. If a person sees clearly that he is going to live on this earth for thirty, eighty, or ninety years and then go off to eternal life, it is worth the trouble to embrace the Cross of Christ in this world, because the Lord is waiting for us in eternal life.—Of course, another of the pillars on which I [might otherwise] have built my convictions, my life, and my existence comes tumbling down.—We Christians cannot stop preaching eternal life, because as the letter of Saint Paul to the Corinthians says, "if Christ has not been raised, your faith is futile" [1 Cor 15:17], and we would be the most foolish of men. I believe in the resurrection and life everlasting, and I know that I am not foolish to believe in them and preach them.

The fact that the authorities are considering the need for a discussion at the national level prompts the following question: Is marriage something that can be made subject to majority opinion?

Your question calls for an affirmative answer, and the truth cannot be determined by majority vote. The Holy Father, the Pope, in his encyclical *Veritatis splendor*, speaks of the great danger that lies in wait for democracies when they introduce majority opinion or consensus as a criterion, apart from the truth. It would be good to remember this sentence from the encyclical and to take it into account: the truth is above all majorities.

There are others who have warned about a built-in despotism in relativism.

Yes, one more than fifty percent impose their point of view on those who are not the one more than fifty percent and who can be right.

In that sense, does the eventual approval of a law on divorce mean an imposition on those who believe in indissolubility?

It is something that introduces a crack in the ground upon which the Christian concept of marriage builds. Undoubtedly, when society lives in an atmosphere in which marriages are dissolved with the blessing of the state, the Christian life becomes even more countercultural.

Some have suggested the possibility of applying the grounds for annulment in canon law to civil law. Do you think this is viable?

It does not seem to me to be a solution. I am prepared to study it and reflect further on it, but to me it does not seem to be a solution for several reasons. First, because the application of grounds involves jurisprudence, that is to say, the tribunal or court interprets the particular grounds [for annulment]. Let us suppose that the grounds for annulment in canon law were copied in a law concerning civil marriage. This does not automatically mean that the jurisprudence of the ecclesiastical tribunals will be copied, so that this same method of applying the law would obtain in the civil courts. So, in my judgment, that does not work. To put it another way: it is not certain that the criterion used by civil judges would be the same as the one used by ecclesiastical judges. And if there are civil judges who hand down civil annulments of marriages now, knowing that those marriages are not invalid, it could happen that there would also be civil judges who would accept a canonical ground for annulment that did not apply either. Besides, this raises another problem. Suppose that two persons who were married in the Church turn to the civil courts to have their marriage annulled on one of the grounds that is identical to those in canon law. The judgment by the civil court is not valid in the eyes of the Church, but these two persons would then come to the ecclesiastical tribunal, or to the bishop, and tell him: "Look, my marriage has been declared null by a civil court on the same grounds that the Church considers sufficient, so just sign here, please, and everything is settled." For the Church, this would create a quite a few problems. Besides, the introduction of divorce creates a very serious problem from a canonical standpoint. When two persons are married in the Church, supposing that they give limited consent, that consent, canonically speaking, is invalid. In other words, if two persons contract marriage conditionally: "I am marrying you, but if difficulties arise that we cannot resolve, then we separate and each one fends for himself", that consent is not matrimony, and, in the eyes of the Church, it is null. When the state introduces divorce as a possible variable in the civil domain, that is going to influence people who are not well informed in the way that they will think about Christian marriage. They are going to think that they can marry while reserving the possibility of a future divorce. That means that there could be a very great number of ecclesiastical annulments because people would not be entering into marriages that were in fact valid. I consider this to be very serious.

It is also suggested that each couple choose, at the moment of contracting a civil marriage, whether they want to accept the rule of indissolubility or not. What are your thoughts on that?

This hypothetical arrangement is not acceptable to me because, as I said at the beginning, indissolubility depends not only on the Christian and Catholic faith, but also on the natural law that obliges every human being. Therefore, that would mean that those who wanted to would accept the natural law, and those who did not care to accept it would not, which creates a very ambiguous situation because it implies an approval of optional observance of the natural law. It would mean accepting the existence of two types of marriage, and I believe there is only one type. That is why it is not an acceptable prescription. Once again we would have the problem of applying the name of marriage to something that is not one.

Marriage is not only a contract, but also a social institution, the basic cell of society. What is the significance of making this distinction?

Marriage is a basic given of human nature. I can enter into it or not, but if I do, I have to agree to all of the terms and conditions of this institution. Naturally, when divorce laws are favored, the institution is shaken at its very foundations, and the end result is what we see happening at the United Nations: they cannot even agree on a definition of what marriage or the family is. In other words, we are heading for total relativism!

With respect to the proposed bill that would grant legal equality to legitimate and illegitimate children, how would this initiative affect the family?

The subject is quite complex. On the one hand there are the rights of those who are legitimate [*verdaderamente*] children, but, on the other hand, there are other rights that, in my judgment, one should not disregard. The whole patrimony of a family is generally created by the father, but the work of the mother, her presence as mother and spouse is a *sine qua non* condition for the formation of a family patrimony. If the father, going behind the back of his lawful wife and betraying her by committing adultery, sires a child by a woman who has not contributed at all to the patrimonial goods, and that child obtains part of that inheritance, to the detriment of the descendants of the lawful marriage, and at the expense of the contribution by the lawful wife, the problem, as I see it, has only been complicated. I understand that the illegitimate child has rights. But if I were to place myself, hypothetically, in the situation of a couple who has no children, for example, and the patrimony of the family has been created by the husband and the wife, and the husband has four children outside of marriage, then his wife contributed on behalf of the four children conceived in adultery. But these are reflections I am making rather quickly. I do not have a clear answer. I see both sides of the problem. In my life I have always had much respect for natural children [that is, children not born to a lawfully married couple].

The distinguished [Chilean national hero] Don Bernardo O'Higgins was affectionately welcomed in the house of my ancestors, who were his godparents, and I learned in my own family to treat a relative who was a natural child with the same respect due to my other uncles and aunts who were the children of a lawful marriage. So I am not slighting illegitimate children or saying that someone who is not born of a lawful marriage does not deserve consideration. But we must also be very careful that the solution does not undermine the stability, the soundness, and the strength of the family. I am not acquainted with the text of the bill, and I do not know what limits have been set, what precautions have been taken, in legislating in this matter.

The eventual introduction of a divorce law in our country is supported by many women, who argue that it would protect them and the family. Do you agree with these arguments?

The one who is really hurt, when a divorce law is passed, is the wife, and I would be delighted if all the ladies who are the slightest bit in favor of the possibility of divorce would take note of that. This is why I am convinced that when crisis situations arise [in a marriage] one should do everything that is humanly possible to resolve them. I have known of many marriages that were going through very serious difficulties that, humanly speaking, were impossible to resolve. Nevertheless, given the determination of both spouses to do anything to salvage the family unit, the marriage was saved. Consider the situation of separated wives. Look at the emotional and economic conditions in which they are living. It is widely known that when a woman is separated she is approached by many who view her as rejected but available, to put it bluntly. Is that what I want for the women of my country? I believe, therefore, that the immense effort required to save a marriage is a moral imperative. And if, ultimately, it cannot be saved, I believe that there are ways of living that are in conformity with the law of God, entailing great sacrifice, accepting the Cross of Christ, and giving faithful testimony that everything that happens in this world is not what is important; rather, the most important thing is what comes afterward. As the letter to the Hebrews says, "what is seen was made out of things which do not appear", that is to say, eternal life is the reason for my existence.

I am also worried about the problem of a divorce law because statistically it can be demonstrated that in the countries where a divorce law has been approved, an abortion law has followed a short time later. When there are no firm, sound, irrevocable principles in one area, I have no reason to suppose that there will be any in another field. A well-known person who occupies a prominent political position in our country has already said that she is not in favor of abortion, but she declares that the subject is debatable. In other words, after an exchange of ideas she could very well have another opinion. The door is opened. Moreover, I think that if there were ever a divorce law in Chile, it would do enormous damage to Chilean society and cause grave harm in the local Catholic Church and would open the door to other things later on. We are on a slope that could lead to such unbelievable absurdities as those of the European Parliament, which is advocating the legitimatization of homosexuality.

CHAPTER FIVE

On Chastity

I. Introduction

Several current events and indisputably newsworthy developments have convinced me that this is an opportune moment
to send to my diocesan priests a catechetical letter on the
virtue of chastity. The present situation makes it an urgent
matter to publish this document. I issue it as the Bishop of
Valparaiso and, therefore, as the custodian of the doctrine
concerning faith and Christian morals with respect to the
flock that has been entrusted to me. I am exercising, then,
my sacred duty of proclaiming the gospel, in communion
with the Supreme Pontiff and with my brothers in the epis-
copate.

First I will point out some of the facts and developments
that call for clarification on this subject.

An Atmosphere Tainted by Eroticism

It is not necessary to be keenly perceptive in order to realize
that eroticism has gained ground in our society, especially in
the urban media. Pornographic publications, magazines, and
videos are quite freely marketed; the subject matter of films,
"soap operas" [*telenovelas*], and songs frequently has the effect

Valparaiso, Chile, March 19, 1994, Solemnity of Saint Joseph, the most
chaste spouse of the Virgin Mary.

of discouraging people from chaste conduct and marital fidelity; the traffic in sex has grown notoriously, with standardized installations and all sorts of conveniences, and secured by municipal licenses; the conduct of persons who express their mutual sexual attraction without the slightest sense of propriety or decorum in public places; the public sale of contraceptives in quite a few pharmacies and supermarkets; the disconnection between sexual relations and marriage; a certain exaggerated "realism" in verbal expressions, with no regard for modesty; clothing and postures that are not conducive to purity; the absence of morality in sexual conduct; widespread publicity about the scandalous conduct of high-ranking celebrities; tolerance in society for unacceptable conduct. All these are unmistakable symptoms of a profound moral crisis—one that is certainly not restricted to the realm of sexuality, but which takes in many others—and not just of a "cultural change", as it has been called. The recent encyclical of the Holy Father, John Paul II, entitled *Veritatis splendor*, points to this moral crisis; in it the Pope reasserts the fact that there is such a thing as objective morality. *One could describe this situation as a negative cultural change, the root of which is found in the moral crisis.* I would like to add here a very significant fact: the word "chastity" is almost completely absent from the current vocabulary; no one speaks about the virtue of chastity, and I have the impression that it is rare that the subject is ever mentioned explicitly in preaching.

A Weakening of the Appreciation of Chastity among Christians

This is not the place for a detailed analysis of the polls on this subject, but it is clear that, even among Christians and among persons who call themselves Catholic, one can observe a confusion of ideas on this issue. In certain circles of young people, there is a significant percentage who think that premarital relations are legitimate, provided that the premarital sexual activity is "done for love" and is justified as a means of "gaining experience". Irregular unions are acquiring a *status* of acceptability, or even legitimacy, something that produces in children and in the young, little by little, the impression that these arrangements are as legitimate and respectable as marriage. Behind the questioning of priestly celibacy, and the lack of understanding as to its significance, is no doubt the low esteem in which chastity is held, in the particular form of complete continence for the sake of the kingdom of heaven. *Permissiveness, which is the result of a society that considers itself "neutral" in matters of morality, having no clear and objective standards with which to evaluate conduct, tends to support the impression that a type of conduct is automatically respectable and acceptable as long as the majority behaves that way.* "Pluralism" now enters into play, conceived of not only as an affirmation of differences, but also as an impediment to the pronouncement of moral judgments and as a *hindrance to the claim that the truth actually exists*, and not just "my" truth and "your" truth. The vocabulary used, even among Christians, is significant. They speak, for example, about a "couple", and this *ambiguous term* serves to give a tone of legitimacy to situations that are morally unacceptable. Thus two persons who live together as husband and wife without being married are, and present themselves as, "a couple" or as being in a "lasting relationship". Two young people who are thinking of getting married but are already having relations also call themselves "a couple", although the word "couple" can also mean lawfully wedded spouses; in the extreme case it is even applied to cohabiting homosexuals. People speak also about "companions", and that ambiguous expression refers to those who are cohabiting without being married, a situation that is morally unacceptable. It is significant that in certain Christian circles there is *a kind of fear of describing improper sexual acts as "sins"*; one prefers to speak of them as "errors", "weaknesses", "frailties", "mistakes", words that all allow the speaker to avoid the explicit reference to God that every human act should have. How lamentable it is to hear fornication or adultery described as "making love", as if sin could ever be love!

AIDS

As a matter of fact, world public opinion is worried about the emergence of the AIDS epidemic: its advance appears to be uncontrollable, and as of yet there is no effective treatment for it. The issue of AIDS is closely related to that of chastity: in the first place because this contagious disease is spread, in a very high percentage of cases, through sexual contact. Of these cases, a great number occur as a result of homosexual contacts, although there are also cases in which the disease is transmitted through heterosexual relations. The cases are nowhere near as numerous among those who observe strict marital fidelity. From the data that are available, we can state that *conjugal fidelity and chastity are the most effective barriers to prevent the spread of AIDS.* We must also state that the one factor that most contributes to the spread of AIDS is a disordered, unchaste sexual life, an unchaste life, and especially homosexual genital activity. However, it is distressing to observe that the battle against AIDS is being focused on the distribution and use of condoms, which are promoted as "safe sex", completely disregarding any moral judgment upon the sexual activity and disregarding also the percentage of instances, not at all inconsiderable, in which these mechanical devices fail, thus leading to error [about safety]. In a *permissive society* in which people come to think that "education" consists in *avoiding risks*, without worrying about how they are to be avoided, and *without asking themselves the question as to the morality of the means employed*, it would seem that the ultimate criterion is "safe sex", which is the equivalent of "sinning safely". The problem of AIDS cannot be addressed properly unless one stresses the fundamental importance that chaste conduct has in stopping its spread.

Divorce

It would be an oversimplification to say that all marital breakups are caused exclusively by improper sexual conduct on the part of one of the spouses, but it would also be plain ignorance of reality to pretend that conduct contrary to chastity plays no part, or a very small part, in failed marriages. Usually a breakup is the result of various factors, but I consider that among them *a lack of self-control in sexual matters* plays an important role. There are disordered types of sexual conduct prior to marriage that cast a very negative shadow over marital life together, when penance has not been done for them and when one goes on viewing them, immaturely and selfishly, as a "single person's prerogative" and not as offenses against God and against one's own human nature. When an irreversible breakup of a marriage occurs, a new field for the practice of chastity opens up: fidelity to the spouse from whom one is separated—and who, perhaps to a great extent, bears the responsibility for what has happened—is an expression of spiritual nobility that can be very difficult to comprehend for someone who sees marriage as nothing more than an agreement to live together for an indefinite time, "as long as love lasts", as they say.

"Sex Education"

This issue has been and continues to be on the table ever since the Ministry of Education issued two consecutive documents on the subject. These documents, which were designed to seek a "lowest common denominator" were unsatisfactory, providing neither a statement of values nor guidance, precisely because their *"pluralism" prevented them from taking an objective concept of morality as their point of departure.* The first document spoke of "sex education", an ambiguous expression that gave way in the second version to the phrase "education about sexuality", which is certainly better. Nevertheless, *neither the first nor the second version mentioned chastity as an approach suited to mature men and women in the realm of sexuality and genital activity.* No education is possible except on the basis of a correct anthropology. Unless one knows what man is, what his destiny is, what the meaning of his life and works is, it is impossible to design an educational program. A truly human anthropology, which is not merely the product of sociological statistics or psychological observations, has to include, necessarily, education in the field of sexuality, an education *that depends, naturally, upon an integral and complete vision of man,* his nature, his final end, and his activity. The principal merit of the second text lies in the acknowledgment that the family and each educational institution has the *autonomous right to establish educational guidelines in this area.* Education for chastity certainly has an important place in a comprehensive education.

The Year of the Family

Both the United Nations and the Catholic Church proclaimed 1994 as the "Year of the Family". The Church made great efforts during this year to strengthen the Christian family, so that each home might be what it should be according to God's loving designs, which are the wellsprings of man's genuine fulfillment. The efforts of the Church included, of course, catechesis on what marriage is—the origin and foundation of the family—on preparation for marriage, on the fullness of life in the family community, on the family as the primary agent in the Christian education of children, on the religious nature of the family unit, on family crises, and so on.

Well, *chastity is a factor of prime importance in the life of the family.* The time of preparation for marriage must be chaste, the love between spouses must be chaste, the children must find within the bosom of the family suitable conditions for formation in chastity. I do not mean to say that chastity is the only structural element in a Christian family, but one must admit that it is one of its pillars, which complements the others and is complemented by them, for without it the others are incomplete, weakened, and lacking in the organic beauty of that familial community which is based on the internal and external harmony of its members. An atmosphere of chastity and purity in a family dignifies its members and constitutes a prerequisite for perceiving the presence of God in that basic community that is the "domestic Church". The family is the proper milieu for the integral education of the children, and one element of this is, without a doubt, formation in chastity.

The preceding considerations show a concurrence of facts and situations that make sober reflection on chastity opportune, and even necessary. The complex problems presented in these facts will have no adequate solution unless real efforts are made to educate the whole human person, which includes educating him to value and to practice chastity.

II. Those to Whom This Is Addressed

Of course, when a document is written by a pastor of the Church who is speaking in his official capacity, the document is addressed primarily to the Catholic faithful who make up that particular Church, the care of which has been entrusted to him by the Holy Father, the Pope. I am speaking particularly to the ministers of the Church, priests, deacons, and catechists, to parents who are in charge of a family, to young people, and to the means of social communication. Those who are Christians, but not Catholics, can see in this writing an expression of our common faith, based on the Sacred Scriptures, even though they do not agree with us on the importance of the Church's Magisterium. For those who do not share the Christian faith, this document may be of interest, so that they may know what the Catholic Church teaches and evaluate her positions, which sometimes are presented in fragmentary and incomplete form, which is a source of misunderstandings or interpretations that are based on insufficient information.

The virtue of chastity should be of interest to all Christians *because it is an attitude that pertains to the correct formation of anyone who really wants to be a human person according to God's design* and a disciple of Christ. It is not only the virtue of a specific age group or for a particular state in life; it is to be practiced throughout one's life and is as essential for men as it is for women. Nevertheless, it has special relevance during one's youth, both because at this age the sexual impulse presents itself forcefully, and also because adolescence is the period of human life when the personality is formed by the practice of all the virtues, among them the virtue of chastity.

Accordingly, I ask those who read this document to do so while thinking above all about themselves, both *to clarify their concepts and their moral evaluation of actions* and also *to embrace with joy the path of purity* and of the necessary victory over those tendencies which are not consistent with chastity. This focus on ourselves *does not prevent us from observing the reality that surrounds us or from judging it with Christian discernment* and not merely by the criteria of statistical studies and bell curves. Immersed as we are in our surroundings, in a particular culture, in a given society, we have the inescapable obligation to confront reality with the truth and, on that basis, to assert our moral judgment. To find out that something is wrong, and then to say it is wrong, is not Pharisaical but, rather, an act of charity. It would be Pharisaical to point a finger at others, forgetting that we ourselves are fragile, that we too are sinners. But it would be a failure of charity to maintain a complacent silence when confronted with something that is at odds with morality. A Christian who finds himself in the presence of sins committed by others cannot allow himself to be carried away by feelings of hatred or contempt toward the sinner; rather, he should experience a profound sadness at seeing that the image of God is being disfigured in a human person, frustrating the salvific plans of God, our Creator and Redeemer.

The reflection that I propose has the purpose of *providing material for apostolic action.* Every Christian has a mission and is, in some measure, responsible for the salvation of his brethren. Well, the path to salvation starts with the enlightenment of the understanding, which has to be "reformed", so that it can "prove [test and discern] what is the will of God, what is good and acceptable and perfect" (Rom 12:2). In times of confusion, such as those in which we are living, apostolic action needs to be taken in the form of *clarifying ideas and values,* that is to say, through the communication of the truth which "will make you free" (Jn 8:32). We must not view the confusion of ideas nonchalantly, because this is one of the ways in which Satan carries out his work, which was marked from the beginning by lying, deceit, and seduction by means of appearances (Gen 3:1ff.; see Jn 8:44). The deceitful work of the Evil One frequently is hidden under euphemisms, that is to say, seemingly harmless expressions that do not prompt us to reject them, but do conceal realities that are morally condemned. We all know the ambiguity of terms such as "girlfriend", "termination of pregnancy", "couple", "companion", "love", words that all too frequently cover up grave sins. *Calling things by their names and leaving no room for ambiguity is one of the ways of performing a work of truth and, for that very reason, of authentic freedom.*

III. Specifying Some Terms

In the subject that we are dealing with, there are terms with meanings that overlap, meanings that it is advisable to distinguish.

Virginity

This is a concept that originally was understood in a biological sense, indicating the physical integrity of a woman. The daughter of Jephthah bewailed her virginity on the mountains because she considered it a dishonor to die without having given birth (see Judg 11:29–40). Virginity also has a religious sense, and in such a context it means the voluntary renunciation of marriage for the sake of the kingdom of heaven. We are in the presence here of a fact that is rooted in a religious motivation. In this second sense the term is applied more often to women, although in Sacred Scripture itself there are instances in which the term is applied to men who, for religious motives, renounced marriage (see Rev 14:4). The Fathers of the Church wrote treatises on virginity and eulogies about the holy virgins. The Catholic liturgy, both in the Missal and in the Liturgy of the Hours, includes common prayers composed for the celebration of memorials or feasts of saints who were virgins. The Roman Pontifical contains a solemn rite, normally presided over by the bishop, to consecrate virgins to the Lord. The Council of Trent declared that consecrated virginity constitutes in itself a state of life superior to marriage (Sess. 24, Nov. 11, 1563, can. 10). This does not mean that by a vow of virginity a person who has thus consecrated himself is already a saint or is holier than a married person who lives a life of perfection in the married state. Saint Ignatius of Loyola pointed out, as a sign of "thinking with the Church", the attitude of those who praise and appreciate virginity, even though they have not been called by God to serve him in that state (see *Spiritual Exercises*, "Thinking with the Church", rule 4).

Celibacy

The word celibacy also has at least two meanings: one that refers to the simple fact of not having contracted marriage, and a second that looks to the *religious motive* that this fact can have. In some languages the word "celibate" is commonly used as the equivalent of "single" or "unmarried", but this use of the term does not mean the same as "chaste". In Catholic religious usage, the word "celibate" has a religious connotation and refers in particular to the man who, with a view to being ordained a priest in the Latin Church, *solemnly promises to remain unmarried and consequently to lead a life of celibate chastity; other male religious who are not priests profess this form of chastity, as well.* Just as the term "virgin" is usually applied to a woman, the term "celibate" is usually applied to a man. A man can consecrate himself to celibacy after he is widowed or after having led a dissolute life. On the other hand, a woman who has been married, or who has voluntarily lost her virginity, cannot receive the consecration of virgins, but she can promise to practice chastity in the future in the manner of celibates.

Chastity

Chastity is one form of the virtue of temperance, the virtue that consists in mastery over the passions and appetites of our human sensibility so that they do not obstruct the goal of human and Christian life, which is "to live for God", without allowing any created thing to supplant him or to become an end that is independent of him or, in a word, to prevent us from loving him with all our heart, with all our soul, and with all our strength (see Deut 6:5; Mt 22:37). Temperance refers to the right use of worldly goods, and man needs this virtue so that these goods will maintain their status as means in the service of the ultimate purpose of the human being, so that they will never be set up as ends in themselves. When confronted with various temporal goods, human nature, which has been wounded by sin, reacts with vehement urges: desires for money, for power, for glory (or vainglory), for sexual pleasure (see 1 Jn 2:16). *Temperance and chastity help man to abide in the truth of his being and of his ultimate purpose* and thus prevent the disordered appetites from taking on the dimensions of idols and claiming God's place and the love that belongs to him alone. In concrete terms, chastity allows man to *maintain dominion over his senses, while honoring the purpose of sexuality and making sure that it is exercised without detracting from the love of God and without fettering the freedom that belongs to the children of God.*

The virtue of chastity is multiform and has various hues according to man's different states in life. He who truly loves God can also love his neighbor for the love of God and discover in him the face of Christ. What chastity requires of someone who has consecrated his life to virginity or celibacy is different from what it demands from those who are united in lawful marriage or from someone who has the intention or desire of marrying later on. All these forms of chastity have something in common: mastery over the sexual appetite, as an expression of the search for God above all other goods and the search for any good only from the perspective of the search for God and for his love. So chastity is not a negative stance; if it demands renunciation and victory over self, it requires these things *with a view to a supremely positive good: love for God. One is chaste in order to love God.* This is how we should understand the beatitude that proclaims the pure or clean of heart blessed, because they shall see God (Mt 5:8). Someone who is pure, in the broadest sense of the word, is in a position to "see" God, to love him, to tell him truthfully that there is nothing as important as he is, in any situation or eventuality.

IV. The Sources of the Catholic Teaching on Chastity

As in all matters concerning Christian life, Sacred Scripture is an important source for understanding the nature of chastity. The following section will be dedicated to this source. The Fathers and Doctors of the Church have written on this subject. The Magisterium has also made its contribution in various documents, for example, those of the Second Vatican

Council, encyclicals, and, very significantly, the *Catechism of the Catholic Church*, where this matter is treated in several places and especially in numbers 1809, 2337 to 2365, 2380 to 2391, and 2514 to 2533. I cordially invite you to read these texts, which are so rich in doctrine and which constitute an authentic teaching with a view to fostering progress in this area of the spiritual life. I have already mentioned that the liturgy of the Church echoes the theme of chastity, above all in the form of consecrated virginity. The life of the Church has been fertile in producing forms and distinguished examples of chastity and virginity, as is demonstrated by figures such as the virgin-martyrs Saint Agnes and Saint Cecilia; saintly monks; holy penitents such as Saint Augustine; holy widows and widowers such as Saint Francis Borgia and Saint Jane Frances Frémyot de Chantal; [young celibates such as] Saint Aloysius Gonzaga; Saint Maria Goretti, martyr to virginity; and our two [Chilean] compatriots, Saint Teresa of Jesus of the Andes and Blessed Laurita Vicuña. Many incidents in Blessed Laurita's life suggest that she could be enrolled not only with the virgins, but also with the martyrs. Today, as yesterday and as always, the perfect disciple of Christ must put all virtues into practice, and, among them, chastity, according to his state in life.

V. Teachings on Chastity in Sacred Scripture

In Sacred Scripture, teachings about chastity can be found in various forms. Of course, *instances of habitual purity* are described, and there are also passages that inculcate chastity and situate it within the perspective of God's plans. Finally, there are formulas *rejecting* conduct or *mores contrary to chastity*. Quite often these different types of teaching are intertwined with one another, and so there is no easy or natural way to examine them systematically.

The Old Testament

We know that *the moral sense developed and matured gradually* in the people of Israel. In ancient times there appears to have been no censure of certain types of conduct, which later disappeared or came to be described in negative terms. The final stage of this maturation of moral judgment came about only with Jesus Christ and his gospel. We must not forget this.

There are, nevertheless, valuable teachings on marriage and chastity in the Old Testament.

The first reference is in the Book of Genesis (1:27–28; 2:18–25). Sexuality is presented as a *constitutive element of a human being*, as a *work of God*. It is he who creates man and woman, so that they may complement each other and procreate in the unity of marriage, a union so profound that it takes precedence over other familial bonds. Man sees woman, recognizes her as flesh of his flesh and bone of his bones, and declares that a man leaves his father and mother and is joined to his wife, and the two become one flesh. Evident here is *the difference between the sexes as the work of God, the complementary correlation of male with female in their profound union.* The biblical text says that "the man and his wife were both naked, and were not ashamed"(Gen 2:25). Sin had not yet caused the sexual appetite to become disordered, and the love between man and woman was serene and free of concupiscence. Once our first parents sinned, however, the eyes of both were opened, they realized that they were naked, and they clothed themselves (Gen 3:7). *Sin had given rise to disorder*, and this disorder had to be conquered; for this to happen, modesty was necessary, represented here by the use of clothing. Later on, God says to the woman, "your desire shall be for your husband, and he shall rule over you" (Gen 3:16). Relations between man and woman are no longer serene; instead they will bear *the mark of disorder, of concupiscence, and of selfishness.*

In the story of Abraham, there is a profoundly dramatic chapter. It is the one that refers to the destruction of the two abominable cities of *Sodom* and *Gomorrah*, soiled with the sin of homosexuality, which was practiced there with impudence and with violence (see Gen 18:16—19:29). The rejection of homosexual practices is absolute. Those practices were a degradation of sexuality, which expressed the loss of the proper meaning that God had given to it and turned it into nothing more than an "experience of vital strength and power".

Later, at the time of the Sinai Covenant, God gave Moses the *Commandments of the Law* and among them established the precept "you shall not commit adultery" (Ex 20:14; Deut 5:18). In the Book of Leviticus (chap. 18), one can read complementary instructions on the right use of sexuality. These requirements of the "Laws of the Covenant" between God and Israel indicate that sexual morality is not something "private" but, rather, has reference to God and to community life within the people of God.

Before Jacob and his children settled in Egypt, we find an episode that sheds new light on the subject of chastity. A son of Judah, Er, had married a woman named Tamar. Er died without descendants, and so, in order to fulfill the law (Deut 25:5ff.), Er's brother Onan took the widowed Tamar as his wife. According to the law, the offspring that a widow would have by the brother of her deceased husband would be considered the offspring of the deceased; this prevented his line from dying out. Onan took Tamar for his wife, but by no means did he want any eventual son of his to be considered legally the son of his deceased brother, Er. So it happened that, while having relations with Tamar, he would interrupt the conjugal act and spill the semen on the ground. God disapproved of Onan's conduct, which was at the same time selfish with regard to his brother's memory and contrary to nature in his relationship with his wife, and he put him to death (see Gen 38:1–10). The continuation of this account shows how unrefined were the ideas about sexual morality among the Israelites of that time (see Gen 38:11–26), although there were some flashes of clarity.

The encounter of *Ruth* with Boaz, who later on would be her husband (and both are listed among the ancestors of David and of Jesus), is a poem of delicate tenderness and family virtues. Ruth seeks Boaz in conformity with the Mosaic law; Boaz treats her chastely and then makes her his wife (see Ruth 3:1ff.).

Many were the merits of *David* as a religious man and as a ruler. There is, however, a terrible episode of impurity in his life. Scripture says nothing about the intentions of Bathsheba, the wife of Uriah and neighbor of David, in bathing on the terrace of her house. What is certain is that David saw her, desired her, and sent for her. Bathsheba conceived a child by David. David hatched a plot so that the child could be imputed to Uriah, but the plan failed. Then David contrived for Uriah to be killed, and so it happened. Adultery was compounded by murder. God made use of a prophet to reprimand David sternly, and he punished him. *David did penance, and in a psalm he expressed his sorrow and repentance* (2 Sam 11; 12:1–15; Ps 51). The text is *instructive* in many respects. Naturally, with regard to the provocation of someone else's concupiscence. Immediately, with regard to the danger of looking at something that can *arouse passion*. Then, concerning *the consequences of a sin* that one wants to conceal; for instance, what happens today, when a child who has been conceived in sin is condemned to death by abortion so that the truly guilty ones may "salvage their honor".

David was the father of the wise king Solomon. Much was expected of the new king, but lust blinded his heart. Scripture says that he loved many foreign women and clung to them passionately. In his old age, his wives *turned his heart after other gods*, and his heart did not belong entirely to Yahweh, his God, as the heart of his father David had. He went so far as to build temples to the idols of his wives and followed after them (see 1 Kings 11:1–13). In the story of Solomon, marriage appears to be at the service of power or political expediency, and sexuality turns into an idolatry that enslaves man.

There are various teachings about chastity in several Old Testament writings that are the expression of the "*wisdom*" of Israel. These writings belong to different literary genres, the study of which is not pertinent here. The tradition of the Church has seen in these writings an intention that becomes clearer in the light of the New Testament. Of course, the order in which these biblical figures and books are arranged here is not meant to be an exact chronological sequence.

Job, in his bitter plea for justice, says, "I have made a covenant with my eyes; how then could I look upon a virgin?" (Job 31:1), and affirms that his heart has not been seduced by a woman (Job 31:9)—two remarks: about chastity of the eyes and about inner rectitude.

The story of Joseph, one of the sons—the favorite—of the patriarch Jacob, is thought-provoking. Sold by his brothers and bought by an Egyptian potentate, he came to be his master's trusted assistant. Scripture says that Joseph was good-looking (Gen 39:6). The officer's wife felt passion for Joseph, but he refused her, saying, "How then can I do this great wickedness, and sin against God?" (Gen 39:9). The seductress did not take no for an answer and tempted Joseph day after day. The young man was steadfast in his chaste refusal, and the indignant woman took revenge on him, slandered him, and managed to have her husband put him in jail (Gen 39:10–20). The teaching of this passage is rich: it speaks to us about respect for conjugal fidelity, about its religious meaning, about the need to resist seduction, and about the distressing consequences that spite can have. The rest of the narrative about Joseph clearly shows that God did not abandon him.

In the Book of the prophet Daniel, there is a tale, quite beautiful in its literary form and religious message, about the chaste *Susanna* (see all of chapter 13). Susanna, a young, married, rich, and beautiful woman, is the object of the desire of two elderly men who hold lofty positions in the Jewish community in Babylon. They take advantage of their power to solicit her—what would be called sexual harassment today—threatening to slander her so that she would be condemned to death if she did not yield to their indecent requests. Very beautiful is Susanna's reply: "I am hemmed in on every side. For if I do this thing, it is death for me; and if I do not, I shall not escape your hands. I choose not to do it and to fall into your hands, rather than to sin in the sight of the Lord" (Dan 13:22–23). While being led to death because of their false accusation of adultery, Susanna cries out to God, saying, "O eternal God, who dost discern what is secret, who art aware of all things before they come to be, thou knowest that these men have borne false witness against me. And now I am to die! Yet I have done none of the things that they have wickedly invented against me!" (Dan 13:42–43). And God heard Susanna's entreaty. In this narrative there is a mighty lesson: *it is better to die than to sin and offend God*. The sin that was rejected here was marital infidelity. Quite a few women find themselves today in a situation similar to that of Susanna, when they are sexually harassed by a powerful boss on whom their jobs, their livelihoods and that of their families depend. The Christian response will always be that of Susanna.

In the Book of *Tobit*, there are also brief indications concerning chastity. The angel counsels the young man that, when he is about to join with his wife, they should first rise up and pray, to ask the Lord to have mercy on them (Tob 6:18). Tobias fell in love with his kinswoman Sarah and took her as his wife, and on their wedding night they both prayed, saying,

> Blessed art thou, O God of our fathers,
> and blessed be thy holy and glorious name for ever.
> Let the heavens and all thy creatures bless thee.
> Thou madest Adam and gavest him Eve his wife
> as a helper and support.
> From them the race of mankind has sprung.
> Thou didst say, "It is not good that the man should
>   be alone;
> let us make a helper for him like himself."
> And now, O Lord, I am not taking this sister of mine
> because of lust, but with sincerity. Grant that I may
> find mercy and may grow old together with her.
>
> (Tob 8:5–7)

In this narrative, conjugal union is situated within the context of a profound relationship with God. Tobias and Sarah marry in order to fulfill God's plans, and their union is realized in an atmosphere of prayer. There is love between the two, and that love has a physical expression, but Tobias *takes care to purify his intention.* A great lesson for Christians who enter into marriage: the conjugal union is a reality that can be completely understood only from God's perspective.

The Book of *Esther* tells of the trust this young queen has in God and her sincere faithfulness to the God of Israel. In this text, there is one expression that provides food for thought. In her prayer, Esther says to God, "Thou hast knowledge of all things; and thou knowest that I hate the splendor of the wicked and abhor the bed of the uncircumcised" (Esther 14:15 RSV). This very brief sentence has a religious background: *conjugal union with someone who is far from Yahweh cannot be pleasing.* Perhaps we can suppose that this is already a veiled announcement of marriage as the image of the spousal love of God for his people.

It is relevant to our purpose to recall the Book of *Ecclesiasticus*, also called the Book of Sirach. Chapter 9 of this book gives *counsels* that concern the practice of chastity: avoid dealings with prostitutes, looking intently at maidens, and unhealthy curiosity; turn your glance away from a shapely woman, and do not keep looking at the beauty of someone else's wife; avoid familiarity with a married woman, because "many have been misled by a woman's beauty" (Sir 9:3–9). Further on in the same book we read that,

> A man who commits fornication with his near of kin
> will never cease until the fire burns him up.
> To a fornicator all bread tastes sweet;
> he will never cease until he dies.
> A man who breaks his marriage vows
> says to himself, "Who sees me?

Darkness surrounds me, and the walls hide me,
and no one sees me. Why should I fear?
The Most High will not take notice of my sins."
His fear is confined to the eyes of men,
and he does not realize that the eyes of the Lord
are ten thousand times brighter than the sun;
they look upon all the ways of men,
and perceive even the hidden places. (Sir 23:16–19)

The observations made in this sapiential book, composed not
long before the New Testament, contain not only rules of
conduct, but also that affirmation that the *domain of purity is
under the care of God*. In the Book of Sirach, too, as in all of
the Old Testament, there are harsh words condemning the
sin of adulterous women (Sir 23:22–26).

In the Book of *Proverbs* there are teachings about marital
fidelity and chastity. Here are some of them:

For the lips of a loose woman drip honey...
but in the end she is bitter as wormwood. ...
[R]ejoice in the wife of your youth,
a lovely hind, a graceful doe.
Let her affection fill you at all times with delight,
be infatuated always with her love.
Why should you be infatuated, my son, with a
    loose woman? (Prov 5:2–4, 18–20)

Do not desire her beauty in your heart,
and do not let her capture you with her
    eyelashes. ...
Can a man carry fire in his bosom
and his clothes not be burned?
                    (Prov 6:25–27; see also Prov 7:5–27)

This is the way of an adulteress:
she eats, and wipes her mouth,
and says, "I have done no wrong." (Prov 30:20)

All these sapiential texts demonstrate progress in the appreciation of chastity, but there is still a long way to go.

In various passages of the prophetic and sapiential books we find the theme of God's love for his people presented under the image of a betrothal, with no hesitation in describing as adultery the sin of the people who go over to other gods (see Hos 2:4ff.; Ezek 16:3ff.; Jer 2:1ff.; 3:20ff.; and, above all, the Song of Solomon). This image will be carried through into the New Testament (see, for example, Jn 3:29; Eph 5:22–33; Rev 21:2ff.). From this perspective it is possible to understand certain precepts from the Book of Leviticus, in which there is a rather lengthy passage concerning the holiness of the priests of the Old Covenant. Of course this "legal holiness" is not identical with what we now understand by sanctity, but it has, in any case, as its basis the conviction that the priest is consecrated to God and dedicated to the service of worship. With regard to simple priests, it is prescribed they will not take a prostitute for a wife, or a woman who has been defiled, neither shall they marry a woman who has been divorced by her husband (Lev 21:7). As for the high priest, whose person was consecrated with the oil of the anointing of God, it is prescribed that he will take as his wife a virgin (Lev 21:13f.). The Aaronic priesthood appears as a sign of the spousal relationship between God and his people, and thus it prefigures the priesthood of Christ, which is shared by his ministers in the New Covenant.

The theme of chastity appears in the Old Testament refracted through the prism of gradual revelation; God progressively made known the paths of salvation to his people and, in so doing, the sort of conduct that is in keeping with those paths. There is no comprehensive and explicit teaching about chastity but, rather, scattered references that appear here and there, glimmerings that announce the light that will come later on, in the plenitude of time. Those glimmerings are not polemical arguments, but they testify to the convictions of the sacred authors: they are episodes or affirmations that are recorded quite naturally and that help to situate the subject within the religious horizon of Israel. It gives the clear impression that chaste conduct is something worthy that is in keeping with justice and sanctity, that flows from a heart set on God, and that makes true wisdom possible. Chastity is a religious issue, something intrinsically related to the search for God, just as lust is a distancing of self from God, an offense against God, and idolatry.

There is no doubt that the Old Testament does not attain the clarity that will be made present in the New, but it prepares the way for it, announces it, and allows us, in a certain way, to catch a glimpse of it. Little by little, monogamous marriage is reestablished as the norm, but divorce is still tolerated as a possibility, albeit with differing notions as to the reasons that would justify it. Jesus will reestablish the initial statute on marriage and definitively rule out divorce.

The New Testament

The teachings on chastity are more numerous in the New Testament than in the Old. It is possible to systematize them in various ways, each one with its advantages and drawbacks. I am choosing one that seems to me to facilitate reading: first, we will consider the *persons* who stand out because of their virginity or chastity; then, we will review the *teachings* of Jesus; finally, we will record the *statements* that appear in

the teaching of *Saint Paul*, without overlooking a few references to the writings of other apostles.

Jesus was celibate, chaste, and virginal. This statement is
not found in explicit form in the New Testament, but it flows
naturally from it and explains quite a few positions that our
Lord took. Mary was a virgin before the conception of Christ,
during childbirth, and after it; this is how the Church reads
what is recorded in Scripture and how she interprets, moved
by the Holy Spirit, Mary's reply to the angel, "how shall this
be done [the fruitfulness that is announced to her], because I
know not man?" (Lk 1:34, Douay-Rheims).[1] Joseph, the
spouse of Mary, is enlightened by the angel, who reassures
him by letting him know that his wife has conceived by the
work of the Holy Spirit. The Church gives Saint Joseph the
title of "most chaste spouse of Mary", and traditional Catholic spirituality sees in the foster father of Jesus the special
patron and protector of the chastity of consecrated persons,
just as he was the guardian of Mary's virginity. John the
Baptist was celibate, and in his case celibate chastity is practiced within the context of his extreme austerity and solitude.
Saint Paul states that he himself did not marry (1 Cor 7:8),
and his teachings about virginity have the tone of one who
speaks from personal experience (1 Cor 7:25). Catholic tradition has always considered the apostle Saint John the Evange-
list as celibate and a virgin. Perhaps that inner purity and that
consecration of himself explain the depth of his understanding of Jesus and also the fact that the Lord commended to
him, from the Cross, the care of his Virgin Mother.

The resolute and clear stand of Saint John the Baptist
against Herod can be emphasized here. Aware of the sin of
adultery and incest committed by Herod Antipas, who had

---

[1] "How can this be, since I have no husband?" (Lk 1:34, RSV).

taken Herodias, the lawful wife of his half-brother Philip, as his own, the prophet told him frankly that he was not allowed to live with her (Mt 14:4). Thus he testified to marital fidelity and against the lechery of the tetrarch. We know what happened then: the hatred of Herodias for John, the seduction of the petty king by Herodias' daughter, and the death sentence for John — the price of a dance that must have been a polished example of provocation to lust (see Mt 14:6ff.).

Jesus spoke on several occasions about chastity. Sometimes in relation to marriage, other times outside of this context.

In the passage commonly referred to as the Sermon on the Mount, Jesus says, " 'You have heard that it was said, "You shall not commit adultery." But I say to you that *every one who looks at a woman lustfully has already committed adultery with her in his heart*' " (Mt 5:27, emphasis added). Immediately afterward come the figurative references to cutting off one's hand or plucking out one's eye, if that is what would be necessary in order to preserve the Christian life—to avoid an occasion to sin, we would say today. This denunciation of sinful glances is a sign of the interiorization of Christian sanctity with regard to the Mosaic law, and it is an echo of the passages from Job (31:1, 9), and from Sirach (chaps. 9 and 23) mentioned above. Later on, and along the same line of the interiorization of morality, Jesus says that "what comes out of the mouth proceeds from the heart, and this defiles a man. For *out of the heart come evil thoughts, murder, adultery, fornication, theft, false witness, slander. These are what defile a man*" (Mt 15:18–20, emphasis added), and not the act of eating without washing one's hands, as was required by the precepts concerning legal purity in the Old Covenant. These two passages come to be very concrete applications of the principle established in the Beatitude that declares

"Blessed are the pure in heart, for they shall see God" (Mt 5:8). True Christian chastity springs from the heart, from a disciplined, purified heart, in which there is no admixture of twisted motives.

On the subject of marital fidelity we read in the Gospel of Saint Mark:

> And Pharisees came up and in order to test him asked, "Is it lawful for a man to divorce his wife?" He answered them, "What did Moses command you?" They said, "Moses allowed a man to write a certificate of divorce, and to put her away" [see Deut 24:1]. But Jesus said to them, "*For your hardness of heart he wrote you this commandment. But from the beginning of creation, 'God made them male and female.' 'For this reason a man shall leave his father and mother and be joined to his wife, and the two shall become one.' So they are no longer two but one. What therefore God has joined together, let not man put asunder.*"
>
> And in the house the disciples asked him again about this matter. And he said to them, "*Whoever divorces his wife and marries another, commits adultery against her; and if she divorces her husband and marries another, she commits adultery*" (Mk 10:2–12, emphasis added; see also Mt 5:31f., 19:3–9; Lk 16:18; 1 Cor 7:10f.).

Jesus' teaching *restores the original image of marriage*. In doing so, it declares that this pattern is not founded solely upon a sociological or psychological basis, but upon the very will of God. "What therefore God has joined together, let not man put asunder." We are not dealing with a recommendation, as when someone makes a better suggestion without excluding the other alternative, which would be acceptable. No, *Jesus rejects the Mosaic toleration and characterizes a new union as adultery*, that is to say, as unlawful and sinful, because it contradicts the will of God.

The teaching of Jesus on marriage provoked among his disciples a reaction that had little in common with the gospel:

"If such is the case of a man with his wife, it is not expedient to marry." But he said to them, "Not all men can receive this precept, but only those to whom it is given. For there are eunuchs who have been so from birth, and there are eunuchs who have been made eunuchs by men, and there are eunuchs who have made themselves eunuchs for the sake of the kingdom of heaven. He who is able to receive this, let him receive it" (Mt 19:10–12).

The disciples' reaction is not very spiritual. *Jesus takes the opportunity to introduce the theme of renouncing marriage for the sake of the kingdom of heaven*, but warns from the very start that he is entering into a realm that is not comprehensible to human reason alone; rather, it requires, in order to enter into this perspective, a *special gift from above*. What connection is there between renouncing marriage and the kingdom of God? The Gospel text affirms that this relation exists but does not indicate the basis for it. If we read this passage in the light of what follows immediately after, concerning material and familial goods (Mt 19:16–29), we can infer that *the renunciation of marriage—like the renunciation of riches—places the disciple of Jesus in a situation that frees the spirit so as to be more attentive to things that are above*. Although the Gospel does not say so, the existence of men and women who have made this sacrifice is a visible sign, in this earthly life, of the absolute dominion of God.

Related to the previous passage is another, in which Jesus, replying to a Jewish casuistry, says, "*For in the resurrection they neither marry nor are given in marriage*, but are like angels in heaven" (Mt 22:30). With these words Jesus indicates that the marital state belongs to earthly life and shares in its *provisional character*, inasmuch as there will no longer be any place in the life of the kingdom for sexual relations in marriage. This passage can be read as an explication of Matthew 19:10–12, in such a way that the renunciation of marriage has the character, during this earthly life, of a certain anticipation of the blessings of the kingdom.

There are still two more teachings of Jesus concerning chastity. One well-known episode, so full of tenderness and mercy, concerns the sinful woman who washed the feet of Jesus during a dinner to which he was invited by a Pharisee (Lk 7:36–50). She was known to be a prostitute, or at least a woman leading a wanton life. The other account is the one about the adulteress whom the Scribes and Pharisees judged liable to death (Jn 8:3–11). The common feature in both accounts is the mercy of Jesus, who "[has] no pleasure in the death of the wicked, but that the wicked turn from his way and live" (Ezek 33:11). What stands out in the first account is Jesus' statement about this woman that *"her sins, which are many, are forgiven, for she loved much"* (Lk 7:47). This saying of Jesus can be interpreted as teaching that lust is rooted in unloving behavior, in selfishness, in idolatry, and that *its cure can come about only from the love that has the power to put each thing in its proper place*, and to set God above all else, since he is the only one who deserves adoration. Jesus' farewell indicates that the woman "believed" in him, trusted in him, that she availed herself of his mercy, and that her faith was what prompted her to express her love for Jesus by anointing his feet with perfume. This was a confident and profoundly humble love, a daring and silent love.

In the episode of the adulteress, there is a suggestion that sins against chastity are not the only ones, that there are others that are just as serious, and, finally, that the guilty woman's deliverance from death did not mean that she did not have to repent and amend her ways: "Go, and do not sin again" (Jn 8:11).

The mercy of Jesus gives clear expression to a new perspective. Someone who has sinned against chastity can obtain God's forgiveness, just like those who have sinned against other precepts of the law. Here, too, it is possible to hope for the gift of a "new heart", capable of truly loving God and one's fellow men. It is very significant that *Mary Magdalen* was at the foot of the Cross and that she received one of the early announcements of the resurrection: she "saw" the risen Son of God (Jn 20:11–17).

Let us now turn to the *apostolic writings.*

In the Book of the Acts of the Apostles there is a passing reference to chastity. In the so-called "Council of Jerusalem", Christians of Gentile origin are instructed to "abstain from what has been sacrificed to idols and from blood and from what is strangled *and from unchastity*" (Acts 15:29). The mention of unchastity refers most probably to sins in the area of sexuality, especially fornication.

The Apostle Paul finds himself confronted with a pagan world where sins in the area of sexuality abound, though they are not the only ones. In the Letter to the Romans, he records the existence of *atrocious conduct* contrary to nature, such as homosexual practices, and he interprets this abominable situation as a consequence of not having honored God and of serving the creature rather than the Creator (Rom 1:24–27). The Apostle repeatedly denounces sins against the right use of sexuality. In the First Letter to the Thessalonians, he tells them: "[T]his is the will of God, your sanctification: that you abstain from immorality; that each one of you *know how to control his own body in holiness and honor,* not in the passion of lust like heathen who do not know God. . . . For God has not called us for uncleanness, but in holiness" (1 Thess 4:3–5, 7).

In Corinth a grave sin of incest had taken place within the

community; the Apostle condemns it and gives a powerful reason to lead a pure life: "For Christ, our paschal lamb, has been sacrificed. Let us, therefore, celebrate the festival, not with the old leaven, the leaven of malice and evil, but with *the unleavened bread of sincerity and truth.*" He then adds that Christians should not associate with someone who, while calling himself a brother, "is guilty of immorality or greed, or is an idolater, reviler, drunkard, or robber" (1 Cor 5:1–13). In the same First Letter to the Corinthians, Saint Paul affirms that:

> *The body is not meant for immorality, but for the Lord, and the Lord for the body. . . . Do you not know that your bodies are members of Christ?* Shall I therefore take the members of Christ and make them members of a prostitute? Never! Do you not know that he who joins himself to a prostitute becomes one body with her? . . . But he who is united to the Lord becomes one spirit with him. Shun immorality. Every other sin which a man commits is outside the body; but the immoral man sins against his own body. Do you not know that your body is a temple of the Holy Spirit within you, which you have from God? You are not your own; you were bought with a price. So glorify God in your body (1 Cor 6:12–20).

Saint Paul's teaching is not limited to rejecting sins against chastity; he also *advances the positive reasons for being chaste.* At the basis of all his argumentation lies the doctrine that a Christian belongs to God, that *he is a dwelling place or temple of God.* Accordingly, although chastity refers to the right use of sexuality, a person will not perceive its profound significance unless he takes into account man's relation to God, whom man should glorify with all of his being. In the Letter to the Galatians, the Apostle mentions fornication, impurity, licentiousness, and other sins as "works of the flesh" and warns that those who do such things *shall not inherit the kingdom of God* (see Gal 5:19–21). The same teaching is repeated in the Letter to the Ephesians: "But immorality and all impurity or covetousness must not even be named among you, as is fitting among saints. . . . Be sure of this, that no immoral or impure man, or one who is covetous (that is, an idolater), has any inheritance in the kingdom of Christ and of God" (Eph 5:3–5).

In the Letter to the Colossians, he returns to the same subject: "Put to death therefore what is earthly in you: immorality, impurity, passion, evil desire, and covetousness, which is idolatry. On account of these the wrath of God is coming [upon the sons of disobedience]" (Col 3:5–6).

Saint Paul does not disapprove of second marriages, after one is widowed, of course (1 Cor 7:39), but when he speaks of the eligibility requirements for bishops and deacons, he demands that they be husbands of only one wife, that is to say, married in only one marriage (1 Tim 3:2, 12; Tit 1:6–9). One can suppose that the Apostle perceives dimly in once-married ministers of the Church a particular reference to the mystery of Christ's love for his Church (see Eph 5:21–33).

The theme of chastity is developed under various aspects in chapter 7 of the First Letter of Saint Paul to the Corinthians. This text is not a "treatise", but rather provides answers to questions that members of that community had asked the Apostle, questions the exact wording of which we do not know (see verse 1). The whole chapter shows clearly that the Apostle considers the area of sexuality to be closely connected with the primordial relationship of every man with God. Saint Paul acknowledges that *both the married state and that of celibacy or virginity are gifts from God* (see verses 7, 17, 28, 38), and that therefore the married state is lawful and sanctifying (verse 14), but he considers consecrated life in virginity or celibacy more commendable for several reasons. First, because *virginity bears the seal of the realities of the kingdom of God in a more evident form than matrimony* (verses 29ff.), which belongs to the "form of this world [that] is passing away" (verse 31). Second, because the *state of continence allows greater freedom for the things that are of God*: "I want you to be free from anxieties. The unmarried man is anxious about the affairs of the Lord, how to please the Lord" (verse 32); the married man, by the nature of things, and because of the obligations inherent in his state, has to be concerned with pleasing his wife, which demands worrying about many transitory things (verses 33–35), and also entails a sustained effort to maintain the proper attitude of the Christian who takes to heart the exhortation of the same Apostle: "If then you have been raised with Christ, seek the things that are above, . . . not [the] things that are on earth" (Col 3:1–2). This endeavor to seek God above all things explains the statement of the Apostle that recommends "let those who have wives live as though they had none" (1 Cor 7:29), which cannot be interpreted as an invitation not to love one's spouse, or to neglect one's duties toward him or her, for that would contradict the Apostle's precise instructions in that same chapter, when he declares the equal rights of the husband and the wife as to the conjugal debt (verses 3ff.), and would fail to take into account the perspective of conjugal love considered as an expression and reflection of Christ's love for the Church (Eph 5:21–33).

The teaching of the Apostle must be understood, then, from an eschatological perspective, with a view to the kingdom. Within this perspective one understands the Apostle's hint as to the possibility of the spouses forgoing conjugal intimacy for a certain time, in order to devote themselves more freely to prayer (1 Cor 7:5). This renunciation must be made by mutual agreement, since otherwise the spouse trying to impose it on the other would be denying his or her right (verses 3f.). The reason the Apostle gives for this abstinence is that it enables spouses to devote themselves to prayer. This reason must be understood in terms of the profound nature of prayer: intimacy with God, placing oneself in the presence of the Absolute. This intimacy demands that the mind be calm, serene, detached as much as possible from disturbances and distractions, and this inner peace is fostered by abstaining from marital relations. In the not-so-distant past, the ritual of the matrimonial blessing included, at the end of the ceremony, an exhortation to sexual abstinence during penitential seasons and on the vigils of important feasts: this was a faithful echo of Saint Paul's teaching. In any case, the Apostle understands that virginity and the renunciation of marriage are ways of life that are not feasible for everyone: "But if they cannot exercise self-control, they should marry. For it is better to marry than to be aflame with passion" (verse 9). This passage has to be understood in light of the earlier verse: "But each has his own special gift from God, one of one kind and one of another" (verse 7).

When we read Saint Paul in this way, we also understand what he means when he says that the married man "is divided" (verse 33), and that, if he recommends virginity, it is in order to encourage us to seek "that which is decent and which may give you power to attend upon the Lord without impediment" (Douay-Rheims verse 35). The word "decent" here does not mean that marriage is "indecent" but, rather, that virginity is above marriage since it pertains to the world of ultimate realities, to the kingdom of God, when women will no longer take a husband, nor men a wife (Mt 22:30). "Division" does not mean that the married Christian can place his or her spouse at the same level as that which belongs to God, but rather that the state of continence promotes freedom of the spirit and dedication, even in terms of time, to the things of God—a "full time" dedication, as we would say today.

Chapter 7 of the First Letter of Saint Paul to the Corinthians assumes that *a spiritual appraisal of marriage and virginity requires subtle nuances and that this can be done only within the perspective of Christian life as a whole, of the particular vocation and grace granted to each individual*, and of the final realities of the kingdom of God.

Before we conclude this survey of the New Testament passages that speak about chastity, we should consider two of them that are of particular interest.

Saint Paul says to the Christians of Corinth: "I feel a divine jealousy for you, for I betrothed you to Christ to present you as a pure bride to her one husband" (2 Cor 11:2). Here we find the explanation of the relationship of the Church—and in her, of each Christian—with Christ the Bridegroom. The broad context of this biblical passage refers to faith in Christ as the only Savior, who frees us from the slavery of sin by his grace and not by our works. The Church is "betrothed", and what she owes her Spouse is a faithful love that puts him in a place that no one can claim to share. The "chastity" and the "virginity" of the Church are the expression of her love and of her fidelity. Viewed from this perspective, *Christian chastity appears as an expression of love for Christ*. It is quite significant that the Apostle chooses it as a privileged expression of Christian love for God. This preferential option of the Apostle, expressed also in the Letter to the Ephesians, explains (together with a number of other passages in Scripture) that "spousal" key to Christian spirituality, a key characterized by tender love and delicate faithfulness.

The Book of Revelation speaks of a group of "[one] hundred and forty-four thousand who had been redeemed from the earth . . . for they are chaste [*in Greek,* virgins]; it is these who follow the Lamb wherever he goes: these have been redeemed from mankind as first fruits for God and the Lamb, and in their mouth no lie was found, for they are spotless" (Rev 14:3–5). The passage, like the entire book, is highly allegorical. *Virginity here is the symbol of faithfulness to God* and of a refusal to worship the idols of this world. Lust is a symbol of idolatry. When the passage is understood in this way, it is clear that those who are "virgins", that is to say, truly worshippers of God and jealous of his glory, are those who can follow the Lamb "wherever he goes" and "had his name and his Father's name written on their foreheads" (verse 1). Again, we see here the correlation between the vocabulary of chastity, in the form of virginity, and fidelity to God and to Christ. The man who truly loves God with all his heart, with all his mind, with all his strength, has now attained the status of spiritual virginity, from which he looks at Christ as the Bridegroom who sanctifies the Church to free her from all stain and to make her capable of loving him with a clean heart, a free and undivided heart, a heart that is chaste in the fullest sense of the word.

This reading of and reflection upon the texts of the New Testament, no doubt, lead us much farther than do the texts of the Old Covenant. In the New Testament, a powerful light is shed upon every form of chastity, starting with the theme of virginity and the hope for the kingdom of heaven. Thus, once more, "what is seen was made out of things which do not appear" (Heb 11:3), and eternal life is the measure of earthly existence.

VI. Presuppositions for a Full Understanding
of Chastity

It is not easy to understand the profound significance of chastity, especially in a world in which this virtue is scarcely mentioned and is not very highly esteemed. In order to perceive certain things, it is important to create favorable conditions, and this is all the more necessary, the more delicate the object. In order to perceive the identity and delicate environment of chastity, some basic conditions are required.

— *Believing in God*, worshipping him as the one Lord, having the deep conviction that *everything must be referred to him*, and that anything that cannot be referred to him has no value whatsoever. Chastity, as we have seen in quite a few passages of Sacred Scripture, has a profound religious dimension and cannot be fully understood unless one is facing God. It is possible for someone who does not believe in God to understand something of what chastity signifies, but he will never come to appreciate fully its deepest meaning and scope.

— *Believing in eternal life*, being firmly convinced that our earthly existence *is only one stage*—the first, provisional, and passing stage—of our individual life, and that after it comes the second, definitive, and never-ending stage, when we shall attain *the fullness of our being* and of our destiny.

— Believing that our *earthly life* has its full meaning only *in terms of eternal life*. These are not two juxtaposed realities, one independent with respect to the other; rather, the first is the path, the instrument, and the preparation for the second, the means to the end.

— Living and thinking with *purity of heart*, for someone who does not live in conformity to what he thinks ends up thinking according to the way he lives. It is difficult for a person who is not living a chaste life to come to have a great appreciation for chastity. Someone who leads a life given over to innuendo and lust is not in a position to understand what chastity is.

— Believing that sexuality is *a work of God*, which has a purpose that is not only biological but also spiritual, and that the use of it must be determined by that finality and must never be detached from it.

— Keeping in mind that human nature, which is a work of God, *is wounded by original sin*. This means that there is within it a disorder in the appetites, which produces impulses that tend to make themselves autonomous and which lead to actions that are not consistent with the final purpose of human nature. When he is aware that he possesses a "wounded" nature, man is able to comprehend that his rule of conduct cannot be to "let himself be carried away" by his impulses, as though they were always good, but rather that he must be alert and vigilant, exercising the control of his reason, illumined by faith, over his appetites.

— The Christian knows that in every human action *the grace of God intervenes*, that mysterious but nonetheless real force that impels him to act in conformity with the will of God, healing the disorder caused by original sin and personal sins, returning man to that loving intimacy with God, and refashioning in the creature the image and likeness of his Creator. The grace of God exerts its influence both on our intelligence—making it possible for us to judge according to the wisdom of God—and also on our will, enabling it to impose its decision upon our disordered appetites, and to will only what God wills.

These seven "presuppositions" should not be viewed as links in a chain, such that each link is derived from the previous one, and the preceding link can dispense with the one that follows; rather, they are facets of the same comprehensive reality, aspects that are interdependent, such that you cannot do without any one of them without endangering the balance and harmony of the whole.

These reflections show that chastity cannot be understood correctly except *in connection with the Christian life*. It is one virtue, among others: *it is not the only virtue, nor can it be understood in isolation from the others*. The "spiritual organism" is a delicate equilibrium in which distinct faculties operate in such a way that each one drives the rest and depends on the others. To think that one can be a Christian without appreciating and practicing the virtue of chastity would be as fanciful as to think that a disciple of Christ could be content with being chaste while overlooking the other virtues. Currently, it would seem that it is more common for people to think that they can be good Christians without loving and practicing chastity.

VII. Concupiscence

The word "concupiscence" belongs to the language of the Bible. Saint Paul tell us that "sin . . . wrought in me all kinds of covetousness. . . . I delight in the law of God, in my inmost self, but I see in my members another law at war with the law of my mind and making me captive to the law of sin which dwells in my members" (Rom 7:8, 22–23).

It stands to reason that the Apostle recommends to Christians: "Let not sin therefore reign in your mortal bodies, to make you obey their passions" (Rom 6:12). Saint Peter admonishes us to flee "from the corruption that is in the world because of passion" (2 Pet 1:4) and warns us of the punishment in "the day of judgment, and especially [upon] those who indulge in the lust of defiling passion" (2 Pet 2:9–10). Saint James teaches that "each person is tempted when he is lured and enticed by his own desire. Then desire when it has conceived gives birth to sin; and sin when it is full-grown brings forth death" (Jas 1:14–15). Saint John the Apostle, in the context of the negative connotations that he commonly employs when he uses the word "world", says that "all that is in the world, the lust of the flesh and the lust of the eyes and the pride of life, is not of the Father but is of the world. And the world passes away, and the lust of it; but he who does the will of God abides for ever" (1 Jn 2:16–17). The "world" in this context is all reality under the power of Satan and his deceits, and Saint John says of him that "the whole world is in the power of the evil one, . . . [whereas] we are in him who is true, in [God's] Son Jesus Christ" (1 Jn 5:19–20).

All these passages illustrate Jesus' warning in the parable of the sower, when he points out, as one of the reasons that the word of God does not bear fruit in some people, "the cares of the world, and the delight in riches, and the desire for other things, enter in and choke the word" (Mk 4:19). That is why the Letter to the Galatians presents the Christian life as a valiant struggle between the spirit and the flesh, warning us that the spirit and the flesh have antagonistic, irreconcilable desires, in such a way that those who truly belong to Christ Jesus have crucified the flesh in "its passions and desires" (Gal 5:16–24). This struggle and the effort to master our urges involve perseverance and self-denial: "Every athlete exercises self-control in all things. They do it to receive a perishable wreath, but we an imperishable. . . . I pommel my body and subdue it, lest after preaching to others I myself should be disqualified" (1 Cor 9:25–27).

Surely, when Jesus says "If any man would come after me,

let him deny himself and take up his cross daily and follow me" (Lk 9:23), he is including the struggle against the internal disorder of concupiscence, and that is how Saint Paul must have understood it when he spoke of having "crucified the flesh with its passions and desires" (Gal 5:24).

The teaching of Sacred Scripture about *concupiscence* makes clear that it *is a disorder*, that it has its origin in sin, that it contradicts the spirit, that it is not in itself a sin but leads to it, and that we must keep up a difficult and ongoing struggle against it.

From reading the biblical passages about concupiscence, it appears that, although concupiscence manifests itself in the *sexual appetite* and is frequently mentioned in that context, it does not pertain only to that field (see 1 Jn 2:16). There is also a disordered urge to possess material goods, and there is another in the pursuit of honors or power. In all of these cases we are dealing with a *created good that is intensely desired, and in a disordered way*, to the point where that desire is no longer consistent with the role that that particular good has in God's designs—plans that coincide with the dignity and sanctity of man. It can be said that goods which are desired in a disordered way eventually turn into *idols* that attempt to occupy the place that belongs to God alone. Just as the truth is what sets man in his proper relationship with God, so too, *idols are intrinsically false*, because they proceed from a deception and falsify the relationship with God.

It is appropriate here to make one further analysis concerning concupiscence.

It is, to begin with, an appetite, an inclination of a human being toward an object that presents itself to him as a good capable of satisfying his desire. This appetite makes itself felt before reason has a chance to judge as to the rightness or impropriety of the desire, which can be more or less vehement. In this sense, it is said that concupiscence is "antecedent", or prior. If the judgment of reason determines that the desire is basically right and that, consequently, the will can assent to the desired object, the impulse of the appetite continues to make itself felt and accompanies the movement of the will. It is, then, "concomitant". If the judgment of reason appraises the object as wrong and tells the will that it must be rejected, and the will in fact does reject it, the desire does not then automatically disappear; it continues to incline the subject toward the desired object, even contrary to the judgment of reason and the rejection by the will. This situation requires a human being to struggle and to employ various strategies in order to subdue the appetite, which is neither desired nor consented to, but which is not within his power to dismiss simply by his refusal. This is "consequent" concupiscence.

Every Christian should be aware of the strength that concupiscence has and against which he will have to struggle until the day of his death. *It is a mistake to think that concupiscence is lulled by satisfying all of its appetites*: Christian conduct in confronting it demands asceticism, struggle, and "self-control" (Gal 5:23).

Concupiscence is aroused when it meets something that can be an object of its appetite. It is not always in our power to avoid the presence of things that stimulate our desires, but it is our moral duty to avoid the things that can arouse concupiscence. Christian spirituality speaks of "custody of the eyes" and of the other senses, that is to say, avoiding the presence of, or not fixing the attention upon objects that can set into motion more or less violent desires that are contrary to Christian virtue, to which one might succumb or which could at least pose a risk to purity of heart.

VIII. Chastity Is a Virtue

We should focus now on this Christian attitude of chastity and examine its nature.

Chastity is a virtue. What does this mean? A virtue is a *steadfast disposition to act well*; it is a "habit" that perfects the person who has it, giving him a certain *connaturality with acting well* in the area of that particular habit. Certainly, all acts that pertain to a virtue are meritorious, but there can be occasional good acts without a "virtue" being present, that is to say, without that firm and unwavering disposition to act well at all times.

Virtues are acquired gradually under the influence of God's grace. They are acquired by means of repeating the acts proper to each one: through this repetition the virtue takes root. Together with the repetition of the virtuous acts it is important, in order to attain the virtue, that there be a strong motivation that leads to those acts. In other words, *the interest and the conviction present in the person who wants to acquire a virtue are very important factors in acquiring it.* On the other hand, someone who attributes little importance or value to a virtue will not acquire it by the mere repetition of more or less mechanical acts.

The virtue of chastity is *one form of the virtue of temperance.* Other forms of temperance are moderation in food and drink, regular habits of sleep and rest, generosity in helping those who are in need, austerity in the use of material goods, mortification of the immoderate desire to know the latest news (that is, controlling "curiosity" in the moral sense), simplicity—for each one according to his own state—in one's style of life, clothing, and so forth.

The practice *of chastity is fostered, above all, by fixing our eyes on God,* by repeated acts of love for him, and by seeking him and his glory above all creatures. There is nothing more purifying, nor can anything lead us so surely to the right appreciation and use of the things of this world, than love for God, who is the maker of every creature. In a certain sense, chastity is *a condition and an expression of a true love for God.*

Every virtue is in the first place interior, which means that it is a *disposition of the heart before it is a feature of external conduct.* But, of course, there cannot be a genuine and sincere interior disposition unless it has an outward expression.

Thus chastity manifests itself in various *external acts* that are signs of sensitivity, a right intention, respect, and reverence for God present in his creatures, especially when the sexual urge can tarnish true love.

The positive aspect in the implanting of a virtue cannot be separated from what could be called the "negative" side, which consists of *rejecting* everything that is contrary to the virtue or that can endanger it. This rejection is undoubtedly a "mortification", something that is accomplished only at some expense and that implies a victory, the renunciation of something that is attractive. It is impossible to practice chastity without rejecting what is incompatible with it or what jeopardizes it in one way or another. "*Self-control*" involves various forms of conduct that must demonstrate the mastery of the spirit over the flesh and, ultimately, the preeminence of the love for God over and above any other affection or pleasure.

This overcoming of oneself in this matter of chastity is just one of the many aspects of the self-denial and carrying of the cross that are required of every Christian. There are those who "live as enemies of the Cross of Christ. Their end is destruction, their god is the belly, and they glory in their shame, with minds set on earthly things" (Phil 3:18–19). Such individuals are not true disciples of Christ precisely because they do not carry their cross and do not follow after

Jesus (Lk 14:27). *Mortification is an expression of the awareness that we are pilgrims here below.* "But our commonwealth is in heaven, and from it we await a Savior, the Lord Jesus Christ, who will change our lowly body to be like his glorious body, by the power which enables him even to subject all things to himself" (Phil 3:20–21). On earth, the Cross—sign of the Lordship of Christ—is the instrument by means of which all of our being is gradually subjected to the power of the spirit, thus attaining true freedom, at the same time that it is being liberated from the slavery of sin (Jn 8:34).

This victory over ourselves, so that chastity may take deep root in our heart, is carried out in various ways. First of all, by controlling our eyes, by turning our glance and curiosity away from that which is an incentive to carnal concupiscence. Also, by giving up reading materials and entertainment that send messages contrary to Christian chastity. Obviously, by avoiding words, conversations, or so-called "humorous" expressions from which the sense of purity is absent. Moderation in drinking is especially important for the exercise of chastity, since a man who finds himself under the influence of alcohol loses, at least in part, control over himself in every sense, the sexual urges included. The question of self-control is a delicate one where *caresses* are concerned. We know that there are caresses that are perfectly legitimate and pure, but there are others that are a powerful incentive to impurity. A caress is in itself an expression of affection, of tenderness, but it can be at the same time a stimulus to uncontrolled reactions that, even though they are not directly so intended, lead to temptation. Those who are preparing for marriage, whether at the "courtship" stage or during the engagement, *must be very careful so that the natural desire to express affection by means of caresses does not exceed the boundaries of purity and does not become an occasion of sin,* in either desire or act. No doubt, during the stages that precede marriage as well, the Cross of Christ must be present in the form of overcoming self in ways that keep the affectionate relationship within the bounds that are suitable for *those who are not yet husband and wife* and who, therefore, cannot express their love in the way that is suitable for those who have joined their lives forever in the sacrament of marriage and have become "one flesh" (Mt 19:6 Douay-Rheims). *From neither a human nor a Christian perspective is dating or being engaged the same as being married: those who are preparing for marriage do not have the same duties, responsibilities, or level of commitment as spouses and therefore do not have the same rights.* Christian chastity demands of those who intend to be married, not only that they abstain from the complete sexual act, but also from all intimate caresses that by their very nature arouse the force of concupiscence and can lead to sin, be it only a sin of desire.

The cultivation of the virtue of chastity requires *avoiding whatever may be an occasion of sin.* Among these occasions we can mention certain places and surroundings, specific persons, some friendships. When it comes to being concerned about the implantation and growth of chastity, it is not fair to think only of ourselves, but we must reflect on the harm that our attitudes can cause to other people. Assuming that something does not constitute a danger for me, I must still ask myself whether it might be for others. The provocation of other people's passions is a sin for the one who caused it. *Scandal,* in the moral sense of the word, *is an act that constitutes a stumbling block for someone else along his path to God.* The words of Jesus are severe in this respect: "But whoever causes one of these little ones who believe in me to sin, it would be better for him to have a great millstone fastened round his neck and to be drowned in the depth of the sea.

Woe to the world for temptations to sin! For it is necessary that temptations come, but woe to the man by whom the temptation comes!" (Mt 18:6–7). The extreme gravity of scandalizing a child does not mean that scandalizing a young person or an adult is unimportant. Whosoever causes scandal, placing obstacles on his neighbor's path as he advances toward God, shows that he is not mindful of the fact that his own moral responsibility concerns not only his own person, but also, in a certain way, his brethren. Never can a Christian repeat the words of Cain, "Am I my brother's keeper?" (Gen 4:9). Each one is responsible for the harm that he does to his neighbor by his words, advice, actions, or omissions.

There is still a word to be said about modesty. *Modesty* is the guarantee, defender, protector, and safeguard of chastity. *It preserves the intimacy of the person* and says "No" to displaying what ought to remain covered. It regulates looks and gestures *in conformity with the dignity of persons.* It invites couples to patience and moderation in their conjugal relationship of love. Modesty respects propriety and should inspire one's choice of clothing. It maintains silence or reserve in areas where one senses a risk of unhealthy curiosity. There is a modesty of feelings just as there is a modesty of the body. This modesty rejects, for example, the exhibitionism of the human body that is used in certain forms of advertising that publicize things that are by nature intimate. Modesty inspires a way of living that allows people to resist the lure of current fashions and the pressure of prevailing ideologies. It is a big mistake to think that modesty is a sort of prudery, or the expression of psychological taboos. It is, on the contrary, that delicate sensitivity so needed in an area of human life that is particularly susceptible to the inner disorder that sin brought to man.

IX. The Forms of Chastity

We have already said what chastity consists of; now we should pause to consider some of the forms that it takes. All of them have something in common, but there are also differences.

Chastity during youth frequently includes the prospect of marriage. One of the characteristics of chastity at this stage is *preparing oneself for the responsibilities of the married state* by the practice of self-control and purification of the heart, which enables the young person to love truly, for the love of God, with a spiritual perspective that looks to eternal life.

When the time of youth has passed, and marriage can no longer be said to be within the horizon of what one foresees or wants, chastity takes on the nuance of the *single life*. It is a state of life that *calls an individual in a special way [to witness] to the religious meaning of life*, by integrating solitude into a lifestyle that shows the way to the kingdom.

The chastity of those who have been called to *consecrate themselves to God* in virginity or celibacy includes the renunciation of marriage, not because they despise it, but in order to respond to God's call to live prophetically the kind of life that will be lived in the kingdom of heaven.

Chastity in marriage does not exclude the pleasure of physical intimacy between the spouses but calls for its purification, in order that *selfishness may disappear*, and so that the spouses may always keep in mind the fact that marriage is a reality that will end, whereas love will never end (1 Cor 13:8). The use of marriage must be such as to remain open to procreation.

Chastity in widowhood is the subject of several teachings of Saint Paul (see 1 Tim 5:3–16; 1 Cor 7:39f.). According to the Apostle, someone who is widowed can lawfully remarry, but he can also take the opportunity presented by his state in life to dedicate himself more diligently to the Lord's service.

A special case in the practice of chastity is that of those who, after marrying, have come to be separated. These persons find that, *as Christians, they need to take upon themselves their loneliness* and give up the prospect of a new union, which objectively would be living in adultery. To remain chaste and alone is required by the indissolubility of marriage and, therefore, by the law of God. Any person who finds himself in this situation can be certain that, *if he employs the natural and supernatural means that God places at his disposal, it will be possible for him to live without offending God.* To these persons applies also what Sacred Scripture says: "God is faithful, and he will not let you be tempted beyond your strength, but with the temptation will also provide the way of escape, that you may be able to endure it" (1 Cor 10:13).

In order to live chastely in any one of the forms in which this virtue may be expressed, according to the various states of life and circumstances, it is necessary *to pray*, to maintain a lively *sense of the faith*, to frequent the *sacraments of penance and Holy Eucharist*, to implore the help of the *Most Blessed Virgin Mary*, to practice *self-control* by means of voluntary mortifications, and to live *in constant vigilance* so as not to give in to the mood of permissiveness that surrounds us. It is necessary to *fight against Satan*, who always resorts to deceit and endeavors to persuade us that impurity "is not that bad a thing", that it is something "natural", that purity is an "impossible ideal", that "love" cannot possibly be a sin, that sexual continence is "harmful to your health" and contrary to nature, that God does not pay attention to "trivialities", that "the important thing is to love your neighbor", that there are many good, respectable people who do not life a chaste life, and so on. It is sad to discover that quite a few Christians have a distorted moral judgment when it comes to matters of chastity, precisely because of these fallacies, which in certain circles are considered to be unquestionable truths.

X. The Sins against Chastity

Sins against chastity, just like all other sins, are simultaneously *offenses against God the Creator, against the dignity of man, who was made in the image and likeness of God, and against the spiritual vitality of the Church*, which is harmed by the sins of her members. The law of God is not an arbitrary and restrictive imposition, but rather is the safeguard of man's well-being and of his destiny.

It is possible to sin against chastity, as against any other virtue, by *thought*, by *word*, by *deed*, or by *omission*. It could be added that in this area, as in others, there are sins of *complicity* and *inducement*, that is to say, when someone helps another to sin by offering him cooperation or induces him to sin by means of provocation, bad advice, or bad example.

It is not a pleasant task to make a list of the different types of sins against chastity: it is a list of the serious weaknesses and deficiencies that disfigure the face of Christ in his disciples. Nor is it pleasant for medical doctors to observe the destructive effects of illnesses on the human body, sometimes with repugnant symptoms, but a knowledge of the concrete manifestations of those illnesses is necessary in order to be able to apply the appropriate treatments and to cure them. So too, a Christian needs to know what are the principal ways of offending against chastity, so as to guard against them and also to offer help to those brothers who could be in danger of destroying the divine life within them and of allowing the image of God to go to ruin by making room for impurity in their hearts.

Sometimes a sin against chastity *is at the same time a sin against another virtue*; for example, adultery, which is an offense against chastity and justice; or incest, which also violates family obligations; or other offenses against chastity that are committed with consecrated persons or in a sacred place, and that are also sins against religion; the abuse of minors, which includes scandal; and others besides.

Generally speaking, sins against chastity are called sins of *lust*, which can be defined as the disordered desire for sexual pleasure to which one consents, or the deliberate action of obtaining it unlawfully, apart from the proper ends of sexuality, which are the union of the two persons in lawful matrimony, and procreation within marriage. When the desire for sexual pleasure occurs in marriage, and with the moderation and delicacy appropriate for someone who sees his own body and that of his spouse as members of Christ and temples of the Holy Spirit, there is no disorder and no lust but, rather, acts consistent with God's design and with the mutual duties and rights of a married couple.

Adultery refers to a sexual relationship with a third person, single or married, other than the person to whom one is joined in marriage. If both sinners are joined in marriage to third parties, the adultery is twofold. Adultery can be occasional or permanent; the latter entails the cohabitation of two persons, one of whom has a marital bond with a third person. When we speak of "marital bond" here, we mean the bond that results from an indissoluble marriage. For the conscience of a Catholic, the annulment of a civil marriage or a divorce in no way changes his status as a person married to his lawful spouse, for as long as that spouse lives. Consequently, any other union after the separation has an adulterous character. It is hard to have to say it, but this is the truth that is in keeping with the gospel. Adultery is a very serious sin.

Fornication is the term for the sexual act performed by two single persons, whether it be occasionally or within the framework of an ongoing relationship. Prostitution and cohabitation are variant forms of fornication. Persons who, while intending to contract marriage, perform sexual acts beforehand (which are frequently called "premarital relations"), commit the sin of fornication. The sin of fornication is serious, although to a lesser degree than that of adultery. Sometimes there are fathers and mothers who supply their sons or daughters with contraceptives "to guard against surprises"; in other words, so that they can sin "safely", without any risk. That is not educating a child in a Christian manner. That is cooperating with what is at odds with morality; in other words, complicity in the sin.

Rape is the sexual act carried out against the will of one person, who is compelled by means of violence.

The name *incest* is given to the sexual union of persons who are united by close ties of kinship [or by marriage].

The *sexual abuse of minors* (a form of rape that in Spanish is called *estupro*) is without doubt an extremely grave sin that results, sometimes, in the corruption of those who are its victims.

Auto-eroticism and *masturbation* refer to the solitary act of physically procuring sexual pleasure with oneself.

Pornography makes public real or simulated sexual acts and exhibits them to third persons, generally for the purpose of making a profit.

The sin of *homosexuality* consists in the *performance* of erotic acts with persons of the same sex. When such acts are performed with minors, the gravity of the sin is greater, since it can cause them to be corrupted.

The sad list in the preceding paragraphs is, lamentably, not exhaustive, but it is sufficient to instruct the uninformed about the more common sins against chastity. *Every sin against chastity that is committed freely and with understanding of its malice, constitutes a grave act against the law of God.* The person who sins can have diminished moral responsibility because of various factors, but no attenuating circumstance can make that which is *objectively wrong and sinful* turn into a good and virtuous act.

In cases of sins against chastity, as with other sins, it can happen that they come to be habitual and not just occasional sins. The *habit of sinning* represents an additional calamity because, even though it can lessen one's moral responsibility, it makes it noticeably more difficult to abandon the custom of sinning. Just as virtue facilitates right action and creates a lasting disposition to do good, so too the habit of sin, or vice, disposes a person to do evil and makes difficult a return to virtuous conduct.

Someone who allows himself to be carried away by a habit of sin experiences, even if he does not recognize it by explicit reflection, *the need to justify himself,* and there are many ways of doing so. He will say that his own case is entirely "different" and an "exception"; or that the sin committed "doesn't hurt anybody"; or else he will realize that it is something wrong but put off amending his ways or breaking off the relationship, and so on. The point is that the sin gradually produces a *spiritual blindness* that renders man incapable of seeing things as God sees them. The ultimate stage is reached when the sinner comes to declare that what he is doing "is not a sin for me", thus setting himself up as the arbiter of right and wrong. It is appropriate to recall here the observation made by Paul Bourget at the conclusion of one of his novels [*A Divorce*]: "He who does not live according to what he thinks, will end up thinking according to the way he lives." It is already a major accomplishment, if we have done wrong, to acknowledge the fact, like the publican in the parable (Lk 18:13), without evasions or excuses.

XI. Conversion and Forgiveness

God does not withhold his mercy from any sinner who converts and does penance for his wrongdoing. There are many examples of this in the Gospels, as well as in the history of Christianity. The Church has never ceased to proclaim the mercy of the heavenly Father, which has been obtained for us through the merits of Jesus Christ our Savior. The Holy Spirit is always moving to conversion the hearts of those who have sinned, so that they may reflect upon their miserable state and start on their journey back to the Father's house.

Sins against chastity are no exception when it comes to God's forgiveness. The Lord can and wants to forgive them, provided that the one who has sinned repents.

How do we obtain *God's forgiveness*? Let us try to describe the stages along the road of reconciliation (see the *parable of the prodigal son*, Lk 15:11ff.).

The first step toward conversion occurs when *someone who has done wrong recognizes it and judges* sincerely that he should not have done what he did. Already in this moment the grace of God is present, at this very moment, in the form of the illumination of the conscience. This first step could be summarized with the words "I am a sinner; I have done wrong."

The second step goes further and consists of *repentance*. The judgment "I have done wrong", which is an act of the mind, is joined by an act of the will: "*I reject what I have done; I detest what I did.*" This is what Catholic terminology calls "contrition", defined by the Council of Trent as "a sorrow of the soul and a detestation of sin committed, with the determination of not sinning in the future" (Council of Trent, sess. 14, Nov. 25, 1551, Decree on the Sacrament of Penance, chap. 4).

This "sorrow" for sin is a *sincere regret* that one has committed it. It is not enough for it to be based on purely natural reasons, for instance, the social disadvantages that a particular sin brings with it, or the harm that certain sins can cause to one's health; rather, there must be *sorrow with reference to God*: either because one is now conscious of having despised God's love and of having returned evil for good, or else because sin offends God's law and separates us from him, so that we deserve a penalty.

The sorrow for sin committed looks to the past. What has in fact been done cannot be undone, but it can be *detested*. It is impossible to obtain God's forgiveness if there is no sorrow or repentance, because it would be incongruous to say to God: "Forgive me, but what I did was right." What would God have to forgive me for, if what I did was not wrong?

Conversion also looks to the future: someone who regrets and detests what he has done, *necessarily has to make the resolution not to do it again.* What could it possibly mean to say to God: "Yes, I am very sorry about what I did, but I am going to continue doing it." This is the case of people who are living in sin—the sin of adultery, for example—and try to have a priest absolve them, even though they have no intention of changing their situation. These people *think that the Church can grant sacramental absolution without there being any repentance, and that is a serious error. If a priest would dare to give absolution to a person who does not have the required disposition—however much this person may desire to be reconciled and to receive the Body of Christ—that absolution would be devoid of all fruitfulness: it would not forgive the sins* and, what is perhaps worse, it would give rise to a deception, since it would muffle the voice of conscience and claim for itself a power that God has not granted to it.

The third step is to approach the sacrament of penance, or reconciliation. Now is not the time to explain this sacrament in detail. Suffice it to recall Christ's solemn words to his apostles: "'As the Father has sent me, even so I send you.' And when he had said this, he breathed on them, and said to them, 'Receive the Holy Spirit. If you forgive the sins of any, they are forgiven; if you retain the sins of any, they are retained'" (Jn 20:21–23). This is nothing else than the origin of the power belonging to bishops and presbyters to forgive the sins of *those who have truly repented*, as was just mentioned. The Christian who approaches the sacrament of penance must manifest to the confessor the sins that he has committed, and with which he has gravely offended God. He must state them, not only in general terms, but specifically, without omitting any circumstances that could aggravate them. With regard to serious sins, he must indicate at least approximately the number of times that he has committed them.

The priest forgives sins by virtue of the power that he has received from God. He does not do so by reason of his personal sanctity, or of his knowledge of theology, or of his possible psychological insights, but rather in God's name, as God's instrument, with the heart of a father, of a teacher, and of a judge.

The fourth step, subsequent to the celebration of the sacrament itself, is the *performing of the penitential acts* imposed by the confessor. We must *distinguish between "penitential acts" and the necessary acts of reparation or restitution for the harm caused* to other persons by reason of the sins that were committed. If a man has fathered a child without being married to the mother, he has inescapable obligations to his child and, quite often, toward the mother as well. The subject of reparation or retribution is very complex, and not always as simple as in the case of a theft. The "penitential acts" are another matter: these are acts of prayer, of charity, or of self-denial, the purpose of which is to make reparation to God, who is dishonored and offended by sin, and to strengthen the will and the Christian life of the penitent, so that in the future he may be better prepared to resist temptation.

It is possible that, in spite of sincere repentance and a firm resolution of amendment, a Christian may fall again into some sin. It should not happen, but it does. If this occurs, the one who has relapsed must examine himself sincerely as to whether he took the appropriate measures so as not to sin again: did he pray, did he meditate on the word of God, did he read books that would nourish his spiritual life, did he receive the Body of Christ fervently, did he commend himself to the Virgin Mary, was he determined to avoid those occasions or circumstances that he knew, from experience, would lead him to sin; did he practice self-control? Having made this examination of conscience, he can and should have recourse once more to the sacrament of penance and ask again, with humility and renewed repentance and resolve, for the priest's absolution.

The sacrament of penance not only brings about the forgiveness of sins and reconciliation with God, but also has a *purifying effect on the soul of the Christian.* It progressively cleans away the traces and scars that mar his spiritual countenance and cloud the sight of someone who should be seeking God with all the powers of his soul. For this reason, although the obligation to confess one's sins in order to obtain God's forgiveness refers strictly to serious sins, *the Church recommends that the faithful confess venial sins as well,* and even repeat occasionally, discreetly and without scruples, the confession of past sins that have already been confessed and absolved.

XII. Conclusion

Have mercy on me, O God,
 according to thy steadfast love;
 according to thy abundant mercy blot out my
  transgressions.
Wash me thoroughly from my iniquity,
 and cleanse me from my sin!

For I know my transgressions,
 and my sin is ever before me.
Against thee, thee only, have I sinned,
 and done that which is evil in thy sight. . . .

Purge me with the hyssop, and I shall be clean;
 wash me, and I shall be whiter than snow.
Fill me with joy and gladness. . . .
Hide thy face from my sins,
 and blot out all my iniquities.

Create in me a clean heart, O God,
 and put a new and right spirit within me.
Cast me not away from thy presence,
 and take not thy holy Spirit from me.
Restore to me the joy of thy salvation,
 and uphold me with a willing spirit. . . .

Deliver me from bloodguiltiness, O God,
 thou God of my salvation,
and my tongue will sing aloud of thy deliverance.

O Lord, open thou my lips,
 and my mouth shall show forth thy praise.

(Ps 51:1–2, 3–4, 7–9, 10–12, 14, 15)

What more appropriate words could conclude this reflection, than those which David composed after he had committed adultery and murder and had been reprimanded by the prophet Nathan—words in which he expressed his repentance and his trust in the mercy of God?

May the Lord grant to us all a pure heart, may he wash and purify us all and make our hearts as white as snow, so that we can love him above all things, and love each creature only in God.

PART THREE

"WILT THOU DESTROY THE CITY?"

(Genesis 18:24)

CHAPTER SIX

Pastoral Care for Persons Whose Family Status Is Irregular

I. An Approach to the Concept of "Pastoral"

The adjective "pastoral" is reminiscent of the Bible, calling to mind passages from both the Old and the New Testament. God is the Shepherd of his people (Is 40:10f.; Ezek 34:11–16). Over the course of history, there are men who deserve to be described as good shepherds (Ezek 34:23; Jer 3:15; Is 44:28), and others who are bad shepherds, because they usurp a name that is fraught with dignity, but do not act in a way that is in keeping with it or with the task that it implies (Ezek 34:28; Jer 2:8; 10:21; 12:10; 50:6).

Jesus Christ identifies himself as the Good Shepherd (Jn 10:11ff.) and contrasts his conduct with that of the hirelings (Jn 10:12). Saint Peter calls him "the chief shepherd" (1 Pet 5:4), and this expression could be interpreted to mean "he in whom all pastoral activity has its origin and is rooted". Peter could not forget that Jesus had commanded him to "tend" his sheep (Jn 21:16ff.), that is to say, to look after a flock that did not belong to him or to the other apostles or to their

This text is dated: Rome, January 3, 1997. On this subject see also the document published in 1994 by the Sacred Congregation for the Doctrine of the Faith: "Letter to the Bishops of the Catholic Church concerning the Reception of Holy Communion by the Divorced and Remarried Members of the Faithful"— ED.

215

successors, but that would always be Christ's flock or fold. In a well-known passage from the Acts of the Apostles, Saint Paul addresses the *episcopoi*, to explain that the Holy Spirit has charged them with "feeding", which is the same as "leading" or "guiding" the Church of God (Acts 20:28).

The Shepherd or Pastor of the Church is a servant (Lk 22:27; Mk 10:45; Mt 20:28; Rom 12:7). He does not feed himself, he does not seek his own economic advantages, or applause, or to have "all men speak well of [him]" (Lk 6:26), but understands his task as a service that can extend as far as "laying down his life for the sheep" (Jn 10:11, 17–18). It is no mere coincidence that many shepherds—bishops and presbyters, and quite a few deacons—have sealed their fidelity to their ministry with martyrdom.

It can be said that "pastoral" ministry is a characteristic of ecclesiastical ministry. All ecclesiastical activity, strictly speaking, is by the same token pastoral, whether in a direct and immediate way or indirectly, that is, at the service of other direct pastoral activities. It can also be declared that all apostolic activity is necessarily marked by the seal of pastoral ministry, either because it is always in communion with the lawful pastors of the Church or else because its methods necessarily bear the imprint of the dispositions of Jesus, the Good Shepherd (see especially Jn 10:2–28). These dispositions are: love, patience, personal acquaintance (and not just statistical knowledge), sharing in the fortunes of the fold, courage and a willingness to take risks, seeking what is best for the sheep, taking the initiative in calling and looking for the lost sheep and bringing it back lovingly to the sheepfold, living for the sake of the flock, and being ready, if necessary, to give one's life to defend the fold. If in the Old Covenant the lamb was one of the most frequent victims in the ritual sacrifices, the name "Lamb of God" that John the Baptist applies to Jesus (Jn 1:29, 36) has a mysterious connection with his role as High Priest of the New Covenant, who enters the sanctuary of heaven, no longer taking the blood of animals but his own blood, offered once for all for the forgiveness of sins (Heb 9:12–14). This offering that the Good Shepherd makes of himself is related to the essence of his mission, "to give his life as a ransom for many" (Mt 20:28), since he has come so that his people may have life and have it abundantly (Jn 10:10). Perhaps we could add another hypothesis here. If the members of Christ are his "sheep" and his "lambs", as he is the Lamb of God, one can infer that this expression also alludes to the "religious" and "sacrificial" meaning of Christian life: the Father has chosen us in Christ to "be holy and blameless before him . . . to the praise of his glorious grace" (Eph 1:4, 6), in other words, so that our life may be for God (Rom 14:8; 2 Cor 5:15). The ritual sacrifice is above all an act of worship, of adoration, and of praise, an expression that all things belong to God and that creation ultimately has no other purpose but his glory. The ritual expression follows from the inner "devotion", the attitude of the adoring creature who encounters in the glory of God his own fulfillment, since we have been created "to the praise of his glorious grace" (Eph 1:6, 12, 14).

Thus, pastoral work is the totality of grace-filled actions that confer divine life upon men, "deifying" them, and giving them a share in the "economy", the mysterious plan of salvation that brings them, at the same time, into the joy of the Spirit and into the liturgy, that worship which is in spirit and in truth (Jn 4:23f.; Rom 12:1f.).

Pastoral activities can be classified according to the three tasks the Second Vatican Council often mentioned as a valid and traditional schema: the proclamation of the word of God, the celebration of the Church's liturgy, and the guidance of the community. Three tasks that are, in a certain way, inseparable from one another and interdependent. Three tasks that are "pastoral" because they are activities through which Christ, the Good Shepherd, communicates his life to those who are members of his Body. It must always be kept in mind that all pastoral work springs from the unity of God's salvific plan and points to that final reality in which God will "be everything to every one" (1 Cor 15:28). From this perspective we can appreciate how wrong it would be to parcel out pastoral care, dividing it up into watertight compartments, sealed off from each other, as though it would be possible to carry on an authentic pastoral activity that could dispense with any one of the fields of salvific action, which is not a human work but the manifestation of the divine economy.

II. Qualities of Pastoral Work

Certain qualities could be pointed out that should always characterize pastoral work.

The *first* is that all pastoral action *must be founded on the Christian and Catholic faith and on the teaching of the Church.* Pastoral work proceeds from faith and aims at obtaining grace or increasing it. Faith must be carried over into life, and the Christian life is an expression of the faith. Therefore it is not possible to devise supposedly pastoral activities that would leave out the faith, or that would ignore the essential demands of a life lived in accordance with the gospel in its totality.

An authentically pastoral activity *cannot be selective, emphasizing only certain parts* of the gospel message, but must be "catholic" [from the Greek *kat' holou*], that is, "according to the whole". It will never be permissible to curtail the gospel message so as to make it more easily acceptable for certain individuals, for the simple reason that this would mean gaining acceptance of something that is not the genuine gospel of Jesus Christ.

The *second* quality is that pastoral work implies *leadership*. This demands clear thinking as to the objective that is being pursued and a willingness to accomplish definite priorities, employing the appropriate methods. Leadership presupposes a decision-making authority and involves various levels of *discernment*, in which different people can express freely and reasonably their preferences with regard to the methodological choices that will be made. Leadership is facilitated when the one who exercises it possesses exemplary qualities that, in themselves, are a persuasive force and an invitation to follow. In the Church, the ministry of leadership belongs to bishops in communion with the Pope, and they can communicate to others in varying degrees a share in their duties. The tradition of the Church has always respected the existence of collegial bodies or tribunals side by side with the individual leadership authorities. The aspect of leadership is very much present in the image of Christ, the Good Shepherd.

The *third* quality can be expressed by the word *guidance*. The meaning is similar to that of leadership but has *a nuance of movement* and implies a pilgrimage. He who leads is also on the road: he travels together with those who are being led, shares their search and their desire to advance. The idea of guidance allows for the eventuality that someone, temporarily, may stray from the right path. For the Christian the "path" is not an inert reality but a person: Jesus Christ. He is the way (Jn 14:6) and he is so because he is the example (see Jn 13:15), because he is the rule, and because it is he who sustains the movement of his Church. It is interesting to note that the expression "the way" was one of the names originally given to Christianity (see, for example, Mk 1:2f.; Acts 16:17; 19:9; 22:4; 24:14; Heb 10:20; 2 Pet 2:2).

The *fourth* quality is *advancement*. Pastoral work not only sustains and nourishes values already acquired but also encourages progress, *growth*, the development of life in Christ. Jesus' method of teaching with respect to his apostles and disciples was marked by patience. He did not state all the demands from the outset but helped them to discover gradually the call to perfection and the meaning of the gospel ideal. "Advancement" or "growth" is a dimension that is closely related to "leadership" and "guidance"; each one of them indicates a dynamism that corresponds both to the interior dimension of "living in Christ" and "by Christ" and also to the eschatological dimension that involves living temporal realities as a prelude to and a preparation for life everlasting. A pastoral activity that did not look to eternal life would have no meaning and would not be in conformity with the Catholic faith.

It is good to keep ever in mind that the *goal* of all pastoral action is summarized in the petitions of the Our Father (Mt 6:9–13), or in the introduction of the Epistle to the Ephesians (Eph 1:3–14), or in the Beatitudes (Mt 5:3–12), in the expression of Saint Paul, "for to me, to live is Christ, and to die is gain" (Phil 1:21), or, as he also said, "if we live, we live to the Lord, and if we die, we die to the Lord" (Rom 14:8). The essential objective of pastoral work is that the plan of salvation be realized in each person and in the community, so that we may all be sharers in the unimaginable riches of Christ (see Eph 3:8) and might possess the fullness of joy in the Holy Spirit here and, later on, in glory (2 Cor 4:17f.).

The foregoing discussion serves to show more clearly the nature of pastoral action as ecclesial action and to avoid the danger of viewing it only as a method of planning, which is useful and necessary provided it remains secondary and instrumental in relation to the very essence of pastoral ministry.

III. The Agents of Pastoral Work

Since pastoral work consists of leadership and guidance, it is clear that it involves a responsibility that belongs to those who are "pastors" in the Church in the strict sense of the word, that is, to the Roman Pontiff; to the diocesan bishops, as visible heads of the particular churches; and to the priests associated with them by virtue of their own ordination, who constitute in the diocese one sole priesthood, sharing with the bishop the responsibility for the pilgrimage of the Christian community. The position of the deacons is found in the area of assisting the bishop and the priest in their tasks, a service that is carried out at various levels of pastoral leadership and that is rooted in the grace of the sacrament of Holy Orders.

The possibilities for pastoral action are not exhausted by the ordained ministers, even though they are the ones who exercise the office of Christ the Shepherd, as his servants and instruments. All Christian believers, by reason of their baptism and confirmation, have an apostolic responsibility: they are sent to give witness to Christ and to his gospel by their words and through their works. Apostolic work is somewhat different from pastoral work, inasmuch as all apostolic work must be carried out in communion with and under the guidance or leadership of the pastors. It can be said that apostolic work is one aspect of pastoral work, is in solidarity with it, and needs—in order to be authentic and fruitful—to be incorporated in the visible, living, and structured organism that is the particular Church. Even though there are many and various forms of the lay apostolate, they all must have a lively sense of unity and catholicity.

Obviously, agents of pastoral action cannot exercise it in an arbitrary manner but only in conformity with the very nature of the economy of salvation, in which the reception of the word of God, sacramental worship, the observance of the gospel law, and the prayer of the Church are indivisibly joined. A "pastoral solution" that would contradict the law of God would not be authentically pastoral, because the plan of salvation cannot be realized apart from the law of God. An approach dictated ostensibly by love cannot contradict the truth, since love and truth are inseparable (Eph 4:15). These considerations underscore the fact that pastoral action is a service: service rendered to God and to his saving plan, and for the same reason, and to the same extent, an authentic service to mankind. If Jesus presented himself as servant (Mt 20:28; Lk 22:27), he performs his service as Shepherd (Jn 10:11ff.), always attentive to the will of the Father (Mt 11:26; Jn 8:29).

Therefore, in pastoral work it is essential to make a continual effort to discern what it is that God wants done: a pastoral "plan" cannot be anything other than an instrument in the service of God's saving plans and never an organizational plan designed according to human criteria alone or with goals that lose sight of that ultimate goal which is salvation and the praise of the glory of the grace of God (Eph 1:3ff.).

IV. Pastoral Care in Difficult and Irregular Family Situations

This kind of pastoral action, like all pastoral work, has as its inspiration the universal salvific will of God the Father, "who desires all men to be saved and to come to the knowledge of the truth" (1 Tim 2:4). Neither the Church nor her pastors nor the faithful can despair of anyone's salvation in this life, and, because of this, there is a pastoral and apostolic duty to come to the help of those who are away from the faith or have strayed from the gospel way of life. The fact that a Christian may live in a state that is objectively sinful does not mean that the Church, who is a Mother, should abandon him. Various sorts of help can be offered: prayer—asking for light, so that the sinner may realize the situation he is in, and strength, so that he may overcome the obstacles in the way of his conversion; counsel; an invitation to meditate on the word of God and to pray; penance on behalf of the person who has distanced himself from the Lord, and so on. A child of God cannot help feeling profound sorrow at the sight of a brother who has gone astray; it would be an unchristian attitude to view moral evil as something inevitable, as something that does not affect us; a man's sin has repercussions, not only for him but for the entire Body of Christ, which is the Church. The saints grieved and wept for the sins of others; they prayed for sinners and had great zeal for their salvation.

We should *distinguish carefully between "difficult" situations and those that are "irregular"*. A "difficult" situation is not in and of itself "irregular"; on the other hand, every "irregular" situation is automatically "difficult".

Among "difficult" situations are those that *Familiaris Consortio* lists in numbers 77, 78, and 83:

— Families of migrant workers;
— families of those who are obliged to be absent for long periods of time;
— families of prisoners, fugitives, and those in exile;
— families without shelter;

— single-parent families;
— families with members who are handicapped, alcoholic, or addicted to drugs;
— families that are ideologically divided;
— families that live within a foreign culture;
— families that live in a locality where they are in a religious or ethnic minority;
— families started by underage spouses;
— families with elderly members;
— families that started with mixed marriages;
— families of those who are separated and divorced but not remarried.

It is clear that all these types of families need the support of effective pastoral action on the part of the whole Christian community into which they ought to be incorporated. The "difficulties" of these families, in general, do not necessarily originate in a moral problem, although they can occasionally be the consequence of actions that were, at that time, sinful. Pastoral action on behalf of these types of families is not the subject of these reflections.

In the category of "irregular" are included various situations that *in and of themselves are inconsistent with morality* and that are, therefore, *objectively sinful*. These situations not only arise from choices that are made contrary to morality, but each one *objectively constitutes a "state of sin"*, a life of sin. Awareness of the immorality of their situations varies greatly from one person to the next and depends on many factors, which sometimes, to some extent, are beyond the person's control.

Familiaris Consortio lists several situations:
— Persons who live together in "*trial*" or "*experimental*" unions ("marriages") (no. 80);
— those who cohabit in *de facto free unions* (no. 81);

— Catholics *joined by civil marriage only* (no. 82);

— those who, having contracted a canonical marriage, have resorted to divorce and entered into a new civil union ("marriage"): these are *"divorced persons who have remarried"* (no. 84).

With respect to these persons, one can *distinguish two things*: in the first place, apostolic and pastoral works *on behalf of* these persons, activities aimed at putting them in touch with some of the means to salvation and, prior to that, making these means acceptable and even desirable to them; and, in the second place, the *participation* of said persons in the apostolic, pastoral, and cultural activities of the Church.

Both types of activity usually encounter a *basic difficulty*, which consists in the fact that quite a few people who find themselves in the aforementioned situations do not consider that they are "irregular", much less that they themselves are living in a "state of sin". Some of these persons will justify themselves by citing "reasons of conscience" or by supposing that Church law concerning marriage is not obligatory in extraordinary cases such as theirs must be. Others admit that it would be a good thing to "regularize" their situation, but think that such "regularization" refers to the legal and social aspects, but not—or not so much—to the aspect of conscience.

From this basic obstacle springs a subjective attitude that makes any solution at all very difficult, and it is this: since these persons do not recognize that their situation is objectively a state of sin, they do not see why they should have to repent. It is understandable that a couple would have great psychological difficulty accepting the fact that a union in which there has been generosity, shared sacrifices, children who have been raised in the Catholic faith, "fidelity" between the parties, mutual support in various acts of seeking

God, the witness of a life lived together that is humanly "fulfilling" and respectable and even accepted by others, by Catholics, as well—that this union is actually under the sign of sin and demands conversion and penance. It is understandable that the Tridentine definition of contrition as "a sorrow of the soul and a detestation of sin committed, with the determination of not sinning in the future" (DS 1676) is difficult for these persons to accept, especially if they understand it as a complete and utter rejection of each and every incident that has been woven into the fabric of a union that was "irregular" to begin with and continues to be so per se. In the dialogue with these persons, a very subtle analysis will have to be made, which is not something easily accomplished, in which the parties manage to *distinguish the sin itself*, which is always detestable and unacceptable, *from certain consequences of it*, which are not bad in themselves and in which they may even rejoice, because they are positive evidence of God's saving plans.

In pastoral care for these persons, *patience and a gradual approach* are, of course, particularly important, not so as to say that what was bad before is now good but, rather, to allow those who find themselves in these situations to start discovering the joy that penance and reconciliation can bring. For these persons the words of Saint Paul to the Romans may have special significance: "We know that in everything God works for good with those who love him" (Rom 8:28). Saint Augustine had no qualms about adding the phrase: "even sins".

The moment when these persons acknowledge that their situation is sinful usually does not occur during the initial stages of pastoral and apostolic work on their behalf. Generally, this moment presupposes a maturity in which knowledge of the word of God and of the Church's doctrine play an important part. For that very reason, pastoral care and apostolic work for them do not have the sole purpose of making them recognize that their situation is inconsistent with the law of God: that realization, though certainly necessary, will be the *result of an interior process of maturing* that, it is hoped, *will take place along similar lines and at the same time in both of the Christians* who are "joined" in an irregular union.

It is quite possible that these persons have built for themselves a system of self-justification that allows them to live in a relative "peace" of conscience. This system is usually an "*accommodation of principles*", a fulfillment of the lapidary observation by Paul Bourget at the conclusion of his novel *A Divorce*, when he says that "He who does not live according to what he thinks, will end up thinking according to the way he lives."

In any case, it is clear that there is a different conceptual basis for each of the several types of irregular unions and, because of this, there will have to be a different [pastoral] approach for each, so as to help individuals set out on a path that leads to an understanding that is in keeping with the Christian faith concerning marriage and, consequently, to a change in their living situation.

V. Concrete Steps

So far we have examined the prerequisites for pastoral action, but this does not mean that nothing can be done until all of these prerequisites are in place. On the contrary, there are many things that can be done and that will have an influence on the eventual resolution of the problem, which is the co-existence of [1] a union that cannot be recognized by the Church as a true marriage, either sacramental or natural, because it is definitively contrary to the law of God, and of [2] a subjective desire to live religiously in peace with God and with the Church.

The Apostolic Exhortation *Familiaris Consortio* indicates, in number 84, a range of possible actions that can be considered both from the perspective of pastoral work "on behalf of" these persons and also from the point of view of their "participation" in the life of the Church. The papal document takes as its point of departure the fact that these persons cannot be considered "separated from the Church", and that means that *they are not canonically excommunicated, and that they have not necessarily broken the bonds of faith and of acknowledging the legitimate authority of the Church. Because of their objective situation of being in mortal sin, it is clear that they cannot be admitted to the sacraments unless there is repentance and a subsequent change of life*, as the same article 84 specifies.

The problem of the "participation" of these persons in the apostolic, pastoral, and cultural life of the Church demands that several factors be taken into account.

To begin with, the communion of faith. If this does not exist, cooperation in charitable or promotional activities is possible, but it would be inconsistent to participate in what constitutes the very core of ecclesial identity—and always assuming, at the minimum, an attitude of respect for Catholic doctrine, not one of contentiousness or rebellion.

Then, the communion that is expressed in the recognition of the legitimate ecclesiastical authorities, whether at the level of the Church Universal or at the level of the particular Church.

There are areas in which apostolic action is an indispensable requirement of faith, such as the raising of one's own children in the faith so as to introduce them to the sacramental life, even when the parents themselves cannot participate in it. This is an activity that does not only constitute a *right* but is also a *duty*, which has its origin in baptism and confirmation—a duty, the fulfillment of which is pleasing to God, and which acquires a very special significance because of the painful situation in which it is carried out.

There is nothing to stop a Christian, even in "irregular" situations and in an objective state of sin, from bearing witness to the faith when the faith calls for an open profession of belief by the children of the Church. This testimony is required of anyone who has received baptism, and it cannot be disqualified on the grounds that it comes from persons who, in one area of their lives, do not act in a way that is consistent with their faith. This inconsistency may perhaps diminish the value of their testimony in the sight of others but, on the other hand, if the witness is given with profound faith and humility and without any effort to justify oneself, it can, paradoxically, prove to be persuasive.

Participation *in activities that involve, to a greater or lesser degree, an official responsibility in the Church* gives rise to a particular difficulty, because it could be interpreted as a "recognition" of the legitimacy of the situation of said persons, or as though their situation were "acceptable" and not objectively sinful. A Christian who finds himself in this sort of situation should in conscience scrupulously avoid giving the impression that his participation in certain ecclesial activities is a "legitimization" of his irregular situation. If the person's stance comes to take the form of pressuring the Church to have his situation treated *de facto* as a lawful, sacramental marriage, then the Church is confronted with a conduct that contradicts the truth. Even if the individual is not fully aware of its magnitude or of its consequences, it sows confusion and damages communion, which can have no other foundation but the truth.

From a psychological point of view and in terms of appearances, seeing persons who live together in an objectively sinful state and who participate jointly in ecclesial activities is something that will prove to be, for quite a few people and rightly, disconcerting and even incoherent. For this reason it is inappropriate for these persons to perform official duties or to be assigned to ecclesial ministries. It is not that their good intentions are being called into question or that they are being judged "undesirable" persons, but it is essential that the Catholic community not receive ambiguous "signals" or be encouraged to think that a lawful sacramental marriage is an "ideal" that in no way detracts from the "legitimacy" of other unions that are objectively neither lawful nor regular.

Undoubtedly, there is an obligation to carry on a delicate pastoral mission of charity on behalf of these persons, but this mission must not be accomplished at the expense of truth. Furthermore, official positions and ecclesial ministries are not things to which the faithful have a "right" but, rather, responsibilities that are entrusted to them by virtue of the free decision of their pastors, after taking into consideration the need and the common good of the Church. It would be a patent abuse in the exercise of his pastoral ministry if someone in a position of ecclesial authority were to introduce or permit the introduction of ambiguous "signals" with respect to the truth of Catholic doctrine. A solution cannot be truly "pastoral" if it does not comply with the truth. And the truth of moral requirements cannot be measured only in terms of a "general orientation" or of one's "fundamental option", but only with reference to the concrete acts and the individual choices in life.

Here I must state explicitly something that was already implicit in what I have said so far. It is evident that when two persons enter into an "irregular" union, which is to say, in a way that is objectively sinful, it is contradictory and inconsistent to perform, with regard to that union, a liturgical or religious act, whatever it might be. It would be an insult to God to invoke his name and his blessing so as to give an appearance of legitimacy to something that objectively is in serious contradiction to his law and plan of salvation. Such a blessing *would be not only illegitimate*, in going against an explicit ruling of the Church (see FC, no. 84), *but also invalid*, because a morally honest purpose would be lacking. And what is true about blessings applies also to other liturgical or religious acts that, sometimes, are deceitfully requested or obtained. Neither priests nor deacons can allow themselves to become accomplices to this type of acts, which would not only constitute a misuse of their ministry, but would also sow confusion among the faithful and create a false conscience in those who enter into irregular unions, making them appear to be, in some way, legitimate or at least acceptable. And this should not be surprising to anyone, since it is nothing other than the consequence of the "truth" of the situation. To contradict this truth would be to falsify freedom.

The same line of thought leads to the conclusion that it is impossible for these persons to receive the sacraments that presuppose the state of grace as the proper disposition. In the case of the sacrament of penance, this impossibility derives from the lack of conversion, that is, of the disposition that rejects the sin committed and—especially in these cases—makes a firm resolution of amendment. Confession is not only the sincere declaration of one's sins, but also the expression of repentance and of the intention not to sin again in the future. Quite a few people in these situations come to the priest in the confessional or outside it; it is impossible to ignore at least an "incipient" desire, on their part, to be reconciled with the Church. If there is no true repentance and purpose of amendment, however, the priest can do nothing but, with great sorrow, deny absolution. This denial *is not an arbitrary act* but, rather, the objective consequence of a sinful situation that has not changed. The priest confessor is not the "proprietor" of the sacrament, but only its "administrator", and he who administers cannot go beyond the faculties that he has received from his master, the proprietor. An absolution granted in the absence of true contrition and purpose of amendment is not only illicit but radically invalid. To give it is not only an abuse but a deception. It could not be given with a view to "only one Holy Communion due to special circumstances", because the state of serious sin, for as long as it lasts, is incompatible with the reception of the Body of Christ in the Holy Eucharist.

In light of these principles, it follows quite clearly that it is also impossible for these persons to receive the sacrament of the Body and Blood of Christ. This is not a matter of a "penalty" established by a positive ecclesiastical ruling but, rather, of *the consequence of a way of life that is not in conformity with the law of God.* Indeed, where there is an attachment to sin it is not possible to realize simultaneously the eucharistic communion, which implies love of God over all that is created, and the offering of one's life as a sacrifice of praise for the glory of the Holy Trinity. There are persons who, in good faith, beg the priest for "permission" to receive Holy Communion at least once, despite their sinful situation. Many of them suppose that this is the proper procedure, because they think that Holy Communion is forbidden to them by a law of the Church, but not by the will of God. And the problem is that they have no clear or full awareness that their irregular and adulterous cohabitation is actually at odds with the will of God. Even the word "irregular", as it is used in some languages, is interpreted by these persons to mean "something that is outside the normal order", but understanding this "order" to refer to a juridical rather than a moral context. Sometimes it is not perceived clearly enough that a serious sin constitutes a choice that resembles idolatry, because a created reality is put in the place that belongs to God alone. A serious sin *is the opposite of adoration*, and, for that very reason, it is a rejection of one's true status as a creature. That is why receiving the sacrament of Holy Eucharist in the state of sin is a big lie: one makes a sign of adoration and of love, while one's deeds demonstrate the contrary. In this case the sin has the character of sacrilege.

The same reasons lead to the conclusion that these persons cannot fruitfully receive other sacraments, such as confirmation and the anointing of the sick, precisely because the former must be received in the state of grace and the latter requires repentance for sins.

The very nature of certain ministerial acts makes it a contradiction in terms to entrust them to persons who are living in "irregular" situations, that is to say, who frequently commit adultery. Examples of such acts are: the habitual or *ad actum* performance of the role of *lector* in liturgical celebrations, that of *extraordinary minister of the Holy Eucharist*, acolyte, *godparent* at baptism or *sponsor* at confirmation, the role of *extraordinary minister* (other than in a case of emergency) *of baptism*, of *witness*—whether qualified or not—*to matrimony*, or of *presider at a funeral*, as well as those of a more canonical nature, such as *ecclesiastical notary, chancellor of the diocesan curia, financial administrator, member of the finance committee*, or of the *diocesan and parochial councils*, and the holding of *leadership positions in apostolic movements*. It is not appropriate for these persons to participate, jointly, in apostolic activities, because this would contribute to giving the impression of a "legitimization" of their situation. For the same reason it is inappropriate for them to present themselves together, as a "couple", in those churches where the Eucharist is celebrated and where their situation is commonly known.

None of these restrictions can be considered offensive or uncharitable, or seen as an arbitrary refusal or a denial of rights. They are, on the contrary, *the consequences of a state of sin that is publicly known*, which the Church cannot pretend to ignore without being unfaithful to her mission as servant to truth. To pass over these "negative consequences" would be a misconceived charity and a blow to the conscience of the Christian community. This position, which might seem severe, is no different from the one that Saint Paul recommended to the faithful of Corinth: even if it is possible to tolerate the sinful situations of those who have no faith, the sins simply cannot be disregarded in the case of Christians (see 1 Cor 5:9–13).

VI. Conclusion

No one can deny that these situations are extremely distressing. They are painful for the persons directly involved in an "irregular" and objectively sinful state. So they are, too, for the pastors of the Church, who cannot help but grieve about the situation far from the path of salvation that has been created by the living status of these persons. This grief does not arise from having to deny certain forms of participation, but from observing a living situation contrary to the law of God. To make people understand this is not an easy task, and it has to be accomplished with great sensitivity, with heartfelt suffering at seeing the situation of these brothers and sisters, showing them affection, kindness, and understanding, but without disguising the truth.

It is necessary to make them see that they are not "outside the Church", although their situation does not allow them access to the sacraments. The very fact that they desire them is already a sign of communion, albeit insufficient, and of the awareness that they form the instrument the Lord uses to communicate his saving grace. From the psychological point of view, these persons feel the need for the Church to treat them as a Mother who does not reject them, although she cannot give them the means of salvation that their own situation prevents them from receiving, and she cannot grant them a participation in the life of the Church, which, besides being irreconcilable with their situation, would have the very serious consequence of creating confusion about an article of faith, such as the marriage bond, its indissolubility, and its demands (see Mt 5:31f.; 19:3–9; Mk 10:11f.; Lk 16:18; 1 Cor 7:10f.). Although it is difficult to get people to understand it, *the Church cannot renounce her unalterable teaching: that between Christians there is no legitimate marital bond other than the sacrament of matrimony* (see CIC can. 1055 § 2). There are many varied circumstances the pastor of souls must analyze and evaluate, but authentic pastoral care cannot abstract from the truth or accept conduct that would lead the Christian community into error or confusion (see 1 Cor 5:1ff.).

The bishops and priests, and their assistants the deacons, must take special care to maintain a *consistent pastoral approach*, carefully avoiding the disorientation that the faithful would experience if they saw that in some places some principles are applied, while in other places *concessions are made which constitute, in essence, a denial of the principles of morality*, as the Church understands and teaches it. Pastors must be prepared to resist the strong emotional impact provoked by the sometimes tragic situation of persons who live together as though married, but in an irregular union, and they must have clear awareness that to yield on this matter does grave damage to the understanding, on the part of the people of God, of the nature of Christian marriage. Fidelity to doctrine is affected not only when the teachings of the Church are explicitly denied, but *also when attitudes are adopted that imply legitimizing de facto something that is contrary to Catholic doctrine.*

Let us be "sincere in our love", "let us speak the truth in love", as the Apostle says (Eph 4:15), because there is no truth without charity, and no charity at the expense of truth. Difficult, but not impossible. Let no one be asked to act contrary to the faith.